Margaret Bourke-White

Young Photographer

Illustrated by Robert Doremus

Margaret Bourke-White

Young Photographer

By Montrew Dunham

ALADDIN PAPERBACKS

First Aladdin Paperbacks edition 1995
Aladdin Paperbacks
An imprint of Simon & Schuster Children's Publishing Division
1230 Avenue of the Americas
New York, NY 10020

Printed in the United States of America
10 9 8 7 6 5 4 3 2 1

Library of Congress Cataloging-in-Publication Data
Dunham, Montrew.
Margaret Bourke-White, young photographer / by Montrew Dunham. —
1st Aladdin Paperbacks ed.
p.   cm. — (Childhood of famous Americans series)
ISBN 0-689-71785-7
1. Bourke-White, Margaret, 1904–1971—Juvenile literature.
2. Women photographers—United States—Biography—Juvenile literature.
[1. Bourke-White, Margaret, 1904–1971.   2. Photographers.
3. Women—Biography.]   I. Title.   II. Series.
TR140.B6D86   1995
770'.92—dc20
[B]   93-46159

To Bob

I would like to acknowledge my appreciation to Roger B. White for his gracious cooperation, invaluable assistance in locating source materials, and permission to use the childhood diaries of his sister, Margaret Bourke-White; to Henriette Kneller for her expert research assistance; to Mrs. Madge Jacobson for her cooperation; and to Jim Dunham for his help in the search. I wish also to express my appreciation to Time, Inc.; Cornell University, and Case Western Reserve University.

Illustrations

Contents

Books by Montrew Dunham

ABNER DOUBLEDAY: YOUNG BASEBALL PIONEER

ANNE BRADSTREET: YOUNG PURITAN POET

GEORGE WESTINGHOUSE: YOUNG INVENTOR

JOHN MUIR: YOUNG NATURALIST

LANGSTON HUGHES: YOUNG BLACK POET

MAHALIA JACKSON: YOUNG GOSPEL SINGER

MARGARET BOURKE-WHITE: YOUNG PHOTOGRAPHER

OLIVER WENDELL HOLMES, JR.: BOY OF JUSTICE

★ ★ Margaret Bourke-White

Young Photographer

A Birthday
on Flag Day

"HERE I COME! Ready or not!" called Margaret. She turned from hiding her eyes on a big tree while playing a game of hide-and-seek. Cautiously she started to look for her sister, Ruth, and two neighbor girls, Charlotte and Helen, who were playing with her.

For a moment she stood still and glanced all around the yard but couldn't see any signs of movement anywhere. Slowly she walked across the lawn, watching for movements and listening for sounds in nearby hiding places. Stealthily she tiptoed up to some bushes and looked in quickly, but didn't find anyone there.

Soon she heard a muffled giggle behind her. She turned just in time to see her sister Ruth run safely from the other side of the yard to the big tree which was home base. "Free!" shouted Ruth. "I'm home free!"

Margaret kept on looking and soon spotted Charlotte and Helen hiding behind some oak trees. She ran toward them, and they started to run for home base. Charlotte dodged and got past her, but she tagged Helen. "You're It, Helen," she cried joyfully.

Now the girls decided to rest for awhile. Helen sat in a swing which hung from a large branch of an oak tree. The other three girls threw themselves on the ground. Then all of them started to talk and laugh.

While they were resting, Margaret happened to remember that the next day, June 14, would be her birthday. Further, she recalled that it also would be Flag Day. Each year she celebrated her birthday on Flag Day. She smiled as she thought of the flags that people would put out on her birthday. All at once she called out, "Tomorrow will be my birthday."

"Will it really?" asked Helen.

"Yes, I'll be eight years old tomorrow," replied Margaret. Then, just to tease Helen, she added, "Many people will put American flags out on my birthday."

Helen looked at Margaret doubtfully and said, "I don't believe it. People don't put flags out on my birthday."

Margaret laughed and tossed her head. "Well, you just wait and see," she said.

This was the year 1912. The White family lived in a big, comfortable house on the outskirts of Bound Brook, in northern New Jersey. The family included the father and mother, Joe and Minna White, and their three children, Margaret, her older sister Ruth, and her younger brother Roger. Joe White was an engineer and inventor who spent many of his waking hours at a drafting board in his home.

Shortly Charlotte jumped to her feet and said, "Let's start playing again."

"All right," said Helen, climbing out of the swing. "I'm It, so I'll go to the home base tree and hide my eyes."

The three other girls scampered about to look for good hiding places. Margaret ran to her favorite hiding place behind some tall weeds back of the garden. She stooped down behind the weeds and waited quietly. While she was waiting she noticed that the sun was low in the sky and realized that it would soon be dark.

Helen found Ruth and caught her in her hiding place. Then she called loudly, "Olley, Olley, Olsome, all in free!"

Margaret crawled out of her safe hiding

place and ran to join the others. Now Ruth went to the tree to hide her eyes and they started another game. This time Margaret ran to a new hiding place by the cellar door. She stooped down so that she couldn't be seen and shivered as she looked out at the fading daylight. She felt uneasy because she didn't like to be alone in the dark.

Before long Charlotte and Helen streaked from their hiding places and reached home base safely. Then Margaret, who could stand the darkness no longer, shouted, "Here I am!"

Quickly Ruth ran over to Margaret and tagged her. "Now you are It," she cried. "Charlotte and Helen came in safely."

Margaret ran out into the yard with the girls. She looked around at the shadowy darkness. She didn't want to hide in the darkness any more. "All right, I'll be It, but we won't play any more today. I'll be It the next time."

Ruth went home with the other girls and Margaret went in the house. Mother closed the book which she was reading and looked over at Margaret. "Are the other girls still outside," she asked quietly.

"No, Ruth and Helen have gone home with Charlotte to play," replied Margaret.

Mother carefully studied Margaret's actions. She felt sure that she had come into the house because she was afraid to play in the dark. "This is a lovely evening, Margaret," she said. "Let's go outside for a while."

Margaret obediently followed her mother outdoors, where they sat down on the front steps. Mother pointed to the bright stars twinkling in the dark sky, but Margaret didn't seem to be interested. She merely clung to her mother, as if she needed protection. Finally Mother said, "Now that you are nearly eight you shouldn't be afraid in the dark."

Margaret looked up at her mother in surprise. She hadn't wanted her mother to know that she was afraid in the dark. "You're right, Mother," she said. "I know it's silly to be afraid in the dark, but I just can't help it."

"Well, the best thing to do," said Mother, "is to go right out into the dark and find that you have nothing to fear." She took Margaret by the hand and added, "Come on, let's play a game. You run around the house toward the garden and I'll run around the house the other way. Then we'll see where we meet."

Margaret's heart beat fast, but bravely she ran into the darkness. Suddenly back of the house she ran into her mother's open arms. Now she felt good and started to laugh as her mother hugged her tightly.

Moments later Mother said, "You see, nothing hurt you. Now run all the way around the house in the dark by yourself."

This time Margaret was not quite so fearful, but ran as fast as she could through the darkness. When she got back to the starting point, she found Mother there waiting for her. Then for the first time in her life she looked at the darkened world without feeling afraid.

Just now Ruth came running home to join Margaret and her mother. "Let's go into the house," said Mother. "Margaret must go to bed so that she can get up early tomorrow morning to celebrate her birthday."

That night Margaret climbed the stairs in the darkness without being afraid. She ran to her bed on a big upstairs sleeping porch. Calmly she climbed in between the fresh, smooth sheets and turned over to watch the pale moon through the screen. Slowly she went to sleep.

During the night a big thunderstorm arose and flashes of lightning darted here and there in the sky. One clap of thunder followed another and great gusts of wind ruffled the treetops. Suddenly the clouds opened and rain came pouring down. Soon the storm passed and the air felt fresh after being washed by the rain.

Margaret was awakened by the storm but felt

safe and comfortable surrounded by the other members of her family. She closed her eyes and slept to the rhythm of the raindrops pelting on the roof. When she opened her eyes the next morning the sun was shining brightly.

She had a joyous birthday feeling as she dressed and ran downstairs. "Happy Birthday," called her mother.

"Yes, Happy Birthday," added Father.

Mother and Margaret walked out on the front porch to look at the flags waving from porches all along the street. All at once Helen came running toward the house. "Margaret, you were right!" she shouted. "People have put out their flags for your birthday."

Mrs. White laughed. "Yes, Margaret is lucky to have her birthday on Flag Day. That's the reason there are so many flags flying today."

A Baby Robin
for a Pet

"I LOVE springtime," said Margaret as she and her friend Helen walked home from school. She had spent a busy year at school and was looking forward to summer vacation so she could roam through the countryside.

When summer vacation came, she sauntered along trails in the nearby woods. Sometimes she took a book with her and lay down in the shade of a friendly tree to read. Often she sat on an old log and watched the birds flitting about and building nests in the trees.

One day when she was walking near her home, she found a little baby robin which had fallen from its nest. She knelt down beside it to see whether she could help it. Its little beak was spread wide open and its body was barely covered with feathers and down. Helplessly it lay on its side.

Margaret reached down, picked up the baby robin, and cradled it in her hand. Rapidly she carried it home and looked for a cardboard box to use as its home. Then she gently placed it inside and brought some dry grass and leaves for its nest. Just then Mother came into the room. "What do you have there?" she asked.

"A little baby robin which I brought home to care for," replied Margaret. "I found it on the ground and have just fixed it a home in this cardboard box."

"Well, you'll have to hunt around for earthworms for it to eat," said Mother.

Margaret put the box on the top railing of the front porch and went to look for earthworms.

She dug up a fat earthworm from a bare place in the yard and started toward the porch. At that moment Helen came running up the walk. "Can you play with me?" she called. Then she noticed Margaret's dirty hands clutching the earthworm. "Ugh! What do you have there?" she asked excitedly.

"An earthworm," answered Margaret, gaily holding the wiggling worm up for Helen to see.

Helen shuddered and stepped back. "An earthworm!" she exclaimed. "What in the world are you going to do with that?"

"I'm going to feed it to my baby robin," answered Margaret.

"Do you have a baby robin?" asked Helen. "Where is it?"

"It's here in this box," replied Margaret, pointing. "I found it on the ground under a tree. It's too small to fly yet."

She dropped the earthworm into the box and

it slowly crawled into a grassy corner. The little bird fluttered and opened its beak. "That worm is too big for the little robin to eat," said Helen, watching closely.

Margaret got a stick and chopped the worm into little pieces. Then she dropped a small piece down into the robin's wide-open beak. After a few bites the robin settled and nestled down into its new home.

"Now that you have taken care of your bird, will you come and play with me?" asked Helen.

Margaret took one last look at the sleeping robin and said, "Yes, what shall we play?"

"Let's go to the school yard and swing for a while," suggested Helen.

The girls hopped down the steps of the porch and started to walk from the house. "Let's walk along the tops of the rail fences to the school yard," said Margaret.

"I'll bet you can't walk along the top of the

rail fences all the way to the school yard without falling off," challenged Helen.

"I'll bet I can," replied Margaret.

Quickly the girls skipped down the street until they came to a rail fence. Margaret climbed up on the top rail and started to walk slowly, with Helen following her. Carefully she placed one foot in front of the other and balanced herself with her arms outstretched. Soon she began to go faster, but suddenly she started to fall to her right. Quickly she leaned to the left and waved her arms to regain her balance. Then she laughed as she started on.

When they reached the end of this rail fence, they climbed down and ran across the road to another rail fence. Margaret hopped up on this second fence and carefully walked along the top rail with Helen right behind her. Suddenly Helen shouted, "Oh!" and started to fall but managed to balance herself. Margaret turned to look at Helen and almost lost her balance, too. When they reached the end of the fence Margaret felt good because she had walked the entire way without falling off.

"All right," said Helen, jumping down from the fence. "You have won your bet."

The girls ran to the swings and started to swing back and forth. For a while they talked and laughed and had a good time together. Before long, however, Margaret's thoughts turned to the baby robin. She felt that she should go home to look after it. Suddenly she jumped out of the swing and said, "I think we have swung long enough."

"Why stop so soon?" asked Helen.

"Because I need to go home to look after my baby robin," answered Margaret.

The girls walked briskly from the school yard. Soon they came to Helen's home, and Margaret walked on by herself. Along the way she stopped to dig up another earthworm. When she reached home she rushed to the box and fed the earthworm bit by bit to the baby robin.

By now it was nearly time for supper. When Margaret stepped into the house Mother looked at her and said, "Go wash your hands."

After supper Margaret and Ruth helped their mother do the dishes, and Roger played with his toys. Father went to his drafting board to work on a drawing. Later Mother sat in her rocking chair with her mending in her lap.

Once more Margaret went out on the porch to look at her baby robin. She carried the box into the dining room to show the robin to her father. "Take it back to the porch," said Mother. "Father is too busy to be bothered. He is working on a new design for a printing press. As you know, he designs some of the best printing presses which are used today."

Margaret took the box back to the porch

and returned to talk with her mother. "Father surely is buried in his work," she said.

"Yes, he tries to do everything right," said Mother. "When he finishes a drawing, he wants it to be as nearly perfect as possible."

Early the next morning Margaret hurried out to look after her baby robin. She picked up the robin tenderly from its box and carried it to the front yard. There she sat down on the grass, holding it in her hands before her. Soon, much to her surprise, the father robin came flying to her lap to feed it.

Every morning from then on she sat on the lawn with the bird in her lap waiting for the father bird to come to feed it. Usually she had to wait only a few minutes for the father bird to come flying in with an earthworm dangling from his beak. The baby bird held up its head and opened its beak wide, eager to get its breakfast as soon as possible.

One day when Margaret was holding the bird it fluttered its wings and flew a few feet away. Then it turned around and hopped back into her lap. Each day it flew a little farther until one day it flew to a bush at the corner of the yard. There it sat for a few moments and then flew off with a joyous flap of its wings.

Margaret sat on the grass with a mixture of joy and sadness in her heart. She felt happy to have seen the little bird grow strong and be able to fly away. On the other hand, she felt gloomy to think that she probably would never see it again. As she took the empty box back to the porch, tears welled up in her eyes and rolled down her cheeks.

Just then Helen came running up to the porch and noticed Margaret's tear-stained face. "What's the trouble?" she asked.

"Oh, my baby robin just flew away and I'm going to miss it," Margaret replied.

"Well, let's go for a little walk," Helen said. "Maybe that will help you forget that the robin has flown away."

The two girls took a short stroll down the street and back. Helen stopped off at home and Margaret walked on alone. She went at once to look in the box on the railing of the porch. There, happily and unexpectedly, she found the pet robin cosily resting inside. It began to chirp and she started to laugh. She could hardly believe her eyes.

For weeks the robin, now almost fully grown, kept coming back each evening to sleep in its box. Regularly Margaret greeted it and gave it something to eat. She talked to it and it chirped back to her, just as if they were having a good visit together.

A Nature Walk
with Father

BOTH FATHER and the girls were interested in the wonders of nature. One Sunday afternoon, a few years later, Father started out for a walk in the woods. The girls followed him, knowing that he would be pleased to have them accompany him. Always they took along a glass jar in which to bring back any bugs, frogs, or plants which they might find.

Quietly they wandered along a path in the woods. They walked softly, listening and looking for birds and other little animals of the forest. Every now and then they stopped to look at something that attracted their attention.

As they went deeper into the forest, less sunlight came through the green leaves. Only small patches of light showed here and there. The huge dark trees reached skyward, and a pale green undergrowth of small trees and bushes filled in beneath them. The floor of the forest was carpeted with moist, dark brown leaves. Scattered delicate flowers raised their heads proudly through these brown leaves.

Before long Father sat down on a large rock beside an overhanging bush. Margaret ran over and stooped down beside him and Ruth came running up to join them. Both girls waited eagerly to see what he was going to do. Calmly he put his hands beside his mouth and started to whistle softly. He looked about as he whistled again and more softly again.

Suddenly a chickadee fluttered down on the bush, close to Father's head, and started to chirp. "Oh, look!" cried Margaret.

"Hush!" whispered Ruth.

Margaret clapped her hands over her mouth. She was excited but didn't want to scare the chickadee away. She clutched her father's sleeve and pointed to the bird. He nodded but kept right on whistling.

Soon another chickadee flew in for a landing. Moments later several more chickadees flew to the bush. Soon a chickadee on the topmost branch started to sing. Then a smaller chickadee close to Margaret chirped a few notes, almost as if it were talking.

Suddenly Margaret was startled by a movement through the brown leaves by her feet. She caught a glimpse of a snake slithering into the bush and grabbed her father's arm. Father turned to look and merely smiled. "You don't need to be afraid," he said quietly.

He reached down and picked the snake up by grabbing it with one hand just behind its head. Then he stroked its graceful body with his other hand. Margaret stepped back to get away from the smooth, wiggling creature, but Ruth leaned over to watch it closely.

"This is a garter snake crawling through the woods looking for its lunch," said Father. "It is perfectly harmless, except for the worms and toads which it would like to eat."

Margaret came a little closer to see the velvety snake in her father's hands. "Will it bite?" she asked.

"No, it won't bite," Father assured her. "Would you like to pet it?"

She reached down cautiously to touch its wiggling body. "Oh, how beautiful it is," she said, "with its dark green coat and light stripes on its back and sides."

Father gently put the snake down and they walked on down the path. They tarried to look up at the trees and knelt down to admire flowers peeking through the underbrush. They slowed down to watch birds fluttering in the trees and rabbits, squirrels, and chipmunks racing across their path.

Soon Margaret noticed an interesting gray web on the loose bark of a tree. "Look, Father," she cried. "What is this?"

Father stopped to look at a webby mass of eggs on the bark. "This is a deposit of some kind of insect eggs," he said.

"May we take it home?" asked Ruth.

"Yes, if you want to carry it on your hand," replied Father, breaking off the piece of bark and handing it to her.

Margaret ran on down to a swampy pond to look for polliwogs. She knelt down at the edge of the pond and Father came to join her. "What are you looking for?" he asked.

"I'm looking for some polliwogs," she said, "but I don't see any."

Father looked closely at the muddy water. "Well, I don't see any polliwogs either, but here are some polliwog eggs."

"Where, Father?" asked Margaret excitedly.

Father reached down and scooped up a gelatinous mass from the water. "Here they are," he said. "Let me put them into your glass jar to take home."

Father and the two girls now started home with their polliwog and insect eggs. Along the way Margaret happened to see a fuzzy caterpillar clinging to a green leaf. "Oh, look!" she cried. "See this pretty caterpillar."

Father looked carefully at the caterpillar. "Yes, it's a swallowtail caterpillar, which will turn into a beautiful butterfly," he said.

"May we take it home with us?" asked Margaret eagerly.

"Of course," replied Father. "Then maybe you can see how it will turn into a butterfly."

Margaret handed the caterpillar to Father and he tucked it into the side pocket of his jacket. On the way home the girls found several more caterpillars which he put in his pocket. By the time they reached home the red sun was sinking low on the western horizon.

"Mother, see what we have," called Margaret as they entered the house.

The girls put the glass jar of polliwog eggs and the piece of bark with its webby insect eggs on the table. Then Margaret went over to Father and started to pull the caterpillars from his pocket and put them on the table. "We'll have to find special places to keep all these things," said Mother.

Ruth carried the jar of polliwog eggs and the piece of bark with the insect eggs to the back porch. Mother went to the kitchen and got out some small jelly glasses. "We'll put each caterpillar under an upside-down glass here on the windowsill," she said. "You'll have to put a green leaf under the glass for it to eat and a twig for it to climb upon."

That evening Mother got out a book on wild-life and read a description of caterpillars and butterflies to the girls. This description told how a caterpillar attaches itself to a twig and changes into a stage called a chrysalis or cocoon. Then later this chrysalis cracks open and a beautiful butterfly appears. "How wonderful!" cried Margaret. "I hope we get to see all that right here before our eyes."

The next morning the girls went to gather green leaves and twigs for the caterpillars. During the coming days they found more cater-pillars, which they brought to the house to put under inverted jelly glasses. Soon the dining room windowsills were loaded with jelly glasses and caterpillars.

Day after day Margaret and Ruth went to

gather green leaves to feed their caterpillars. One by one they placed the leaves under the jelly glasses for the caterpillars to eat. Much to Margaret's surprise one day, she noticed that a caterpillar was starting to spin a silken thread. "Come quickly, Mother," she called, "to see what this caterpillar is doing."

Mother hurried to the window and knelt down to look at the caterpillar. She noticed that it was spinning and fastening a little silken thread to the twig under the glass. "It's spinning a little silken hammock for its chrysalis to hang from," she explained.

Margaret nodded as she listened and looked. Suddenly she clapped her hands and cried, "Oh, look! The caterpillar's skin is starting to split open."

Mother and Margaret watched as the fuzzy covering of the caterpillar folded back, showing a yellowish-brown chrysalis underneath.

This chrysalis clung gracefully to the twig under the glass. "Now the caterpillar has reached the chrysalis stage," said Mother.

"What will happen next?" asked Margaret. "Will this chrysalis turn into a butterfly?"

"Yes," replied Mother, "but we must watch and wait because only nature knows when the butterfly will be ready to appear."

"Well, I'm going to watch carefully," said Margaret, "because I don't want to miss seeing it when the time comes."

Caterpillars
to Butterflies

FROM DAY TO DAY during the summer life continued much the same in the White family home. Each evening after supper, Father worked busily at his drawing board and Mother sat nearby doing the family mending. The three children spent their evenings reading favorite books, playing with friends or experimenting with their worms, bugs, and insects.

One evening Father planned to stay up beyond the usual bedtime to finish an important drawing. Finally Mother said, "Let's all go on to bed so we won't disturb Father while he works." Soon Mother and the three children were fast asleep in their beds. A few hours later Margaret woke up and heard her father's footsteps down below. She was surprised to find that he was still working and was tempted to tiptoe downstairs to see him. She whispered to her sister, "Ruth, are you awake?"

"Yes," answered Ruth. "Why do you ask?"

"Because I hear Father still working downstairs," whispered Margaret. "Let's sneak down to see him."

Downstairs the girls found Father in the kitchen, drinking a glass of milk. "What are you girls doing up at this hour of night?" he asked in surprise.

"We heard you walking about down here and just came down to see you," said Margaret.

"Well, good," said Father. "I just finished my drawing and was drinking a glass of milk before going to bed. It's time for us all to settle down for the rest of the night."

He led the way from the kitchen in to the dining room. Inside the dining room the girls ran to peek at their caterpillar nursery in the moonlight. Margaret could barely see in the dim light, but she thought she saw a trace of movement under one of the glasses. "Look, Ruth," she cried. "This chrysalis is moving."

Father turned on the dining room light and went over to the window. He stooped down to look carefully. "You are right, Margaret," he said. "This chrysalis is moving."

Margaret knelt down and Father pulled up a chair to watch. Ruth bent over to look and said, "I'll go to call Mother."

Still tying the belt around her robe, Mother came downstairs with Ruth. "Here, Minnie," said Father, giving his chair to Mother and pulling up another for himself. Ruth knelt on the floor by Margaret and they all watched the miracle of the birth of a butterfly.

The moonlight grew brighter as it streamed in the dining room window. Mother turned out the light and everybody watched the opening of the chrysalis by moonlight. "May I take the glass off the chrysalis?" asked Margaret.

"Yes, you may," answered Mother. "Then we can see better."

Carefully Margaret lifted the jelly glass from over the chrysalis on the twig. She could see the dry-looking case wiggle. Then suddenly there was a tear in the chrysalis. Mother, Father, Margaret and Ruth sat speechless as they watched. Magically by the light of the moon, the chrysalis opened and out of it crawled a crumpled, shapeless velvet insect. Margaret drew in her breath. The miracle had happened.

The freshly born butterfly swelled and stretched and changed into a full-blown, beautiful butterfly as they watched. Gracefully it dipped and waved its wings as if testing them.

"Oh, it's beautiful!" cried Margaret as she looked at its black velvety wings dotted with small yellow spots.

All at once another chrysalis began to break open and Ruth said softly, "Look, here's another chrysalis breaking open. Come and watch."

Margaret scooted over by Father where she could see better. As she was moving she noticed another wiggling chrysalis and lifted the jelly glass from over it. One after another, beautiful velvety black swallowtail butterflies emerged from their shells.

The moonlight shadows moved as the night wore on. Mother and Father, Margaret and Ruth watched the butterflies appear.

After a long while Roger, the youngest member of the family, came creeping down the stairs. "Mother, where are you?" he called.

"I'm here watching beautiful butterflies," said Mother. "Come and watch them, too."

By now five or six gorgeous butterflies were clinging to the curtains. Roger's eyes opened wide as he stared at the beautiful creatures. "All of them have come from the caterpillars," explained Margaret happily.

Mother took Roger on her lap and the entire family spent the whole night watching the miraculous births of the butterflies.

The next day Margaret called her friends, Helen and Charlotte, to show them what had happened. They could hardly believe their eyes when they looked at the beautiful butterflies which had come from the ugly little cases on the windowsill. Mother smiled as the girls shared their excitement and new knowledge with their friends.

"It is time now to free the butterflies, Margaret," she said.

Margaret was sorry to have to let the butterflies go, but she knew that they belonged outdoors. "Shall I open the windows to let them out?" she asked hesitatingly.

"Yes," said Mother. "We'll leave the windows open and I think all of them will find their way out."

When Margaret opened the windows, one of

the butterflies gently waved its wings and drifted out. Then one by one the other butterflies flew out into the bright sunshine. One sat on a bush outside the window, gracefully waving its wings. Helen watched excitedly. She shook her head as she said, "I just can't believe that all this would happen."

That fall Margaret attended a different school from Ruth. On the first day she walked to school with her friends, Helen and Charlotte. When they reached the building, they found the principal, Mr. Love, standing at the door. "Welcome back," he said pleasantly. "Your room this year will be Number Eleven."

The girls walked into Room Eleven and sat down with the other pupils. An attractive lady stood behind the teacher's desk. She had soft blond hair and snappy blue eyes. "Good morning, girls and boys," she said cheerfully. "My name is Miss Rugen, and I'll be your teacher this year. We'll start our year's work by sharing some of our summer experiences. Have any of you something interesting to report?"

Helen put up her hand, and Miss Rugen nodded for her to speak. "I suggest that you ask Margaret to tell us about the caterpillars which she and her sister kept at home this summer," she said.

"Good," said Miss Rugen. "Margaret, please tell us about your caterpillars."

Margaret arose and told the full story of how she and Ruth had kept a caterpillar nursery during the summer. Her eyes gleamed brightly as she told how many of the caterpillars had turned into butterflies. When she finished talking Miss Rugen said, "You've had a wonderful experience this vacation."

A short time later Margaret found two little furry caterpillars in the woods. She put them into a box and decided to take them to school.

Miss Rugen looked into the box to see what Margaret had brought. "What cunning little creatures!" she exclaimed.

Curiously she picked up the two fuzzy caterpillars. They curled up into tight little balls in the palm of her hand. "Will they turn into butterflies?" asked a pupil.

"No, but I believe they will turn into tiger moths," replied Miss Rugen.

"May we keep them to find out?" asked Helen.

"Yes, that is a good idea, but we'll have to ask Margaret," said Miss Rugen.

Margaret nodded her head. "Of course you may have them," she said happily.

"Well, we'll have to keep them for several months, because they won't spin cocoons until spring," said Miss Rugen. She pressed her lips together as she thought. "I know what we can do," she added. "We can keep them in the box on the outside ledge of the window. We'll have to cover the box in some way, however, to prevent them from crawling out."

The teacher reached into the bottom drawer of her desk and pulled out a piece of cheesecloth. Carefully she laid the cheesecloth over the top of the box and tied it on tightly with a string. Then Charlotte opened the window and Margaret placed the box on the ledge outside. "Now we'll have to gather leaves and blades of grass to feed them," said Margaret.

"Whenever we feed them we'll have to take the cloth off," said Helen.

"Yes, but that will be easy," said Margaret.

During the coming weeks the pupils brought leaves and blades of grass for the caterpillars to eat. One day when it was Charlotte's turn to feed the caterpillars she noticed that one of them was gone. "Oh, Miss Rugen! We've lost one of our caterpillars."

Miss Rugen came to look. "Yes, one of them has crawled out and probably started for the woods," she said. "Someone must have been careless about tying the cheesecloth on tightly."

Joey, one of the boys in the class, was listening closely. "Well, I fed the caterpillars yesterday and I may have been careless," he said meekly. "I'm sorry if I let one of them get away from us."

"Don't worry," said Miss Rugen calmly, looking at Joey. "We'll just have to take better care of the one we have left."

Soon the weather grew colder and the children didn't have to worry about feeding the caterpillar. It simply stopped eating and rolled itself into a little ball to wait for spring.

Having
Winter Fun

WHEN WINTER CAME, the countryside was covered with snow and the ponds and creeks were frozen over with ice. One cold Friday in January, Margaret awakened to find large feathery snowflakes tumbling to the ground. She couldn't even see the trees at the edge of the garden. "Oh, how beautiful!" she thought.

Downstairs she and Ruth watched the snowstorm through the window as they ate breakfast. After breakfast, Mother brought out a pie tin of bread crumbs and handed them to Margaret. "Here are some crumbs for you to give to the song sparrows," she said.

Margaret stepped out the back door and started to throw the crumbs on the ground. Suddenly she realized that the birds couldn't find the crumbs in the snow and decided to set the pan of crumbs on a nearby stump. "I left the pan of crumbs on the stump where the birds could find them," she said when she went back into the house.

"That was a smart thing to do," said Mother. "The birds wouldn't be able to find them in the deep snow."

"Maybe the snow is too deep for us to go to school this morning," said Ruth.

"Oh, no," said Mother. "Of course you can go to school, but you must wrap up well and wear your overshoes. You'll enjoy walking through the snow in the brisk morning air."

The two girls left for school together. They walked slowly into the wind with their bodies bent forward. As they pushed their feet along, their heavy overshoes plowed furrows in the deep snow. Soon they turned around and walked backwards to keep the heavy flakes from hitting them on their faces. Before long they separated, each to go to her own school.

When Margaret reached school she found only five other pupils in her room. All the others hadn't been able to come because of the heavy snowstorm. Miss Rugen sat down at one of the front desks and all the pupils who were present gathered around her. They talked about the snowstorm and wondered about their little woolly caterpillar asleep in the box outside the window. Later on they played a few games, checkers and anagrams.

In the afternoon Miss Rugen taught them how to make charcoal drawings. Margaret enjoyed using the soft, sooty-black charcoal to make a picture. She drew a scene in the woods with a log sticking out of a pond.

"That's a pretty picture, Margaret," said Charlotte who was sitting beside her.

After school the children tarried for awhile to play on the schoolground. They played a game of fox and geese, chasing one another through the soft snow. Soon Joey picked up a handful of snow and started to make a snowball. Just then Mr. Love came to the door and shouted, "No snowballs, please."

Joey dropped the snowball, but another boy grabbed up some snow and started to wash Joey's face. Everybody laughed and then started to wash one another's faces in the snow.

Mr. Love watched all the fun and finally called, "Now, all of you start home so that you can get there safely before dark."

On Saturday morning Margaret and Ruth planned to go to Lily Pond near their home. There they hoped to spend the afternoon skating with some of their friends. Before the time came for them to leave they helped their mother with her usual morning work.

After breakfast the girls began to clear off the table and do the dishes. Ruth started to wash the dishes and Margaret got out a dish towel to dry them. They sang as they worked, happy to give their mother a helping hand.

Margaret dried the dishes faster than Ruth could wash them. As she waited, she flipped her dishtowel and danced around the room. Soon Ruth placed a large china plate on the drainer. With her towel in one hand, Margaret reached for the plate with the other hand. Suddenly it slipped from her hand and fell crashing to the floor. "Oh!" she cried, jumping back from the broken pieces of china.

Mother rushed into the kitchen to see what had happened. She looked down at the broken pieces of china on the floor and glanced at the girls. "I'm glad neither of you is hurt," she

said. "Did one of you drop the dish accidentally or did you drop it carelessly?"

"Margaret dropped the dish accidentally,"
said Ruth. "It merely slipped from her hands."

"How do you feel about it, Margaret?" asked
Mother.

"I feel terrible," replied Margaret. "I think
I had an accident, but I may have been a little careless, too. I was dancing around and
probably didn't take time to pick up the dish
carefully."

"I am proud of you for telling the truth,"
said Mother, "but still you'll have to be pun-
ished. Ruth can go on to the pond, and you'll
have to finish doing the dishes by yourself.
After you finish drying them put them all away
carefully in the cupboard."

The girls cleaned up the pieces of broken
china on the floor. Ruth left for the pond with
her skates and Margaret washed and dried the

rest of the dishes. After she had put all the clean dishes away in the cupboard she asked, "Now may I go to the pond, Mother?"

"Yes, and I hope you have a good time there," said Mother.

Margaret put on her coat and cap, grabbed her skates, and took off for the pond. When she arrived she sat down on a log at the edge of the pond to put on her skates. Ruth saw her sitting there and skated over to meet her. Then together they went gliding out onto the ice to join their friends.

The group of boys and girls skated around and around the pond. Soon one of Ruth's skates came loose from her shoe and she fell to the ice. Margaret came skating up to her and asked, "Are you all right?"

"Yes, but I can't keep one skate on," answered Ruth. "I think I'll have to go home to have Father fix it before I can skate any more."

After Ruth left the children decided to play hockey. A couple of boys got out some sticks and a puck which they had brought with them. Margaret had only played hockey once before and was especially eager to play again.

The players on both teams skated fast over the ice, chasing the puck. Sometimes it was hard for them to know which way to turn and which way to shove the puck. Margaret was especially happy when she hit the puck with her stick and drove it far down the ice toward the goal. The longer she played the better she understood the game.

The boys and girls laughed as they skated and swung their hockey sticks. Sometimes they hit the stick of another player and missed the puck entirely. Now and then one of them fell down while making a swift stop or turn.

Margaret could skate faster than most of the other players. When she came close to the puck, she could keep hitting it ahead of the others toward the goal. She played so well that her team won the game.

After the game was over she glided to the edge of the pond and sat down on a log to rest. She chuckled to herself when she heard one of the boys say, "Margaret White is a real hockey player. This was only the second time that she has ever played a real game, but she played better than most of us."

Happy Hours on a Coasting Trip

ONE SUNDAY forenoon in winter Mother was busy preparing the noonday meal. She opened the oven door and pulled out a roaster and took off the lid. She quickly glanced at the juicy beef roast and lifted the roaster to the top of the stove. Then she tested it with a fork and said, "The roast is done."

The fragrant aroma of the juicy brown roast filled the entire kitchen. Margaret and Ruth enjoyed the aroma as they dashed about to help their mother. Ruth was setting the table and Margaret was bringing large pitchers filled with water and milk.

Carefully Mother lifted the roast from the roaster and placed it on a large meat platter. Then she carried the platter of meat and several bowls of vegetables to the dining room table and said, "Now everything's ready to eat. Margaret, you may go to call Roger from the living room."

"Roger, it's time for dinner," Margaret said to her brother, who was playing a game on the living room floor. Next she walked over to her father, who was working in the dining room, and said, "Father, dinner is ready."

Slowly Father raised his eyes from his work. "Margaret, do you want something?" he said.

"Yes, I have come to tell you that dinner is ready," she said. She laughed to think that she had to tell him the second time.

Father promptly laid his drafting tools aside. "All right," he said. "I'll come at once."

Soon all members of the family were seated

around the dining room table. Both parents and children enjoyed eating their good meal of meat and vegetables, followed by fruit and cookies for dessert. Mother always tried to prepare a well-balanced meal for her family.

After the meal was over Margaret looked out the dining room window. She saw two little song sparrows nibbling bread crumbs which she had put outdoors for the birds. Ruth came to join her and noticed that it was a beautiful winter day outside. "Father, will you take us coasting this afternoon?" she asked.

Roger was still sitting at the table eating his fruit. He held up his spoon and called, "Yes, Father, will you take all of us coasting this afternoon?"

At first Father, with twinkling eyes, thought he would tease the children a bit. "I'm afraid it's too cold to go coasting this afternoon," he said, winking at Mother.

"It's a perfect day outside," said Margaret. "Even the song sparrows are out."

"We won't get cold," called Roger from the table. "We'll put on our heavy winter clothes to keep us warm."

"Well, there may not be enough snow on the hills for coasting," said Father.

"Oh, yes, there is!" cried Margaret. By now she knew that her father was only teasing.

Father looked at the eager faces of all three of his children. Then he looked over at Mother and said, "I guess I don't have a choice. I'm outvoted in favor of coasting."

Mother laughed. She knew all the time that Father had wanted to take the children. "All right, go on while the sun is high," she said. "I'll look after the dishes."

With much confusion, Margaret and Ruth scrambled into their warm coats and pulled their woolen caps down over their ears.

Quickly they wrapped their long brightly-colored scarves around their necks. Then they ran out the front door to get their sleds. "Hey, wait for me!" called Roger.

The two girls started away slowly, pulling their sleds behind them. Father and Roger followed along behind them, pulling a larger sled. "Where shall we go?" asked Father.

"Let's go to the Watchung Mountains," said Margaret. "The coasting should be very good there with all this snow."

Father had expected this answer. He knew that the children liked to coast on the steeper slopes of the hill-like Watchung Mountains. The girls often went coasting on the lower slopes by themselves.

All of them climbed halfway up the mountain pulling their sleds behind them. Margaret was the first to take off. She lay on her stomach on the sled and went sliding down safely all the way to the bottom. Quickly she rolled off and pulled her sled to one side to get out of the way of the others.

Ruth came coasting down the hill next. After her came Father and Roger riding on the big sled together. Roger sat in front and held tightly to the rope to guide the sled down the hill. "Look," Margaret called to Ruth. "Roger is steering the sled by himself."

Now all of them slowly pulled their sleds halfway up the hill again. By now several other boys and girls had come to the mountain to coast and they had to take turns with them. Once more Margaret lay down on her stomach on her sled and grabbed the steering bar with both hands. "Do you want me to give you a shove?" asked Ruth.

"Yes, please," answered Margaret. "Give me a good fast running start."

Ruth put her hands on the back of Margaret's

sled and pushed it along for several steps. Margaret kept her head up to watch where she was going. She steered her sled carefully and shot past several other sleds going down the hill. When she reached the bottom she quickly scooted her sled out of the way of other sleds coming down the hill. Then she waited until Ruth, Father, and Roger reached the bottom with their sleds. Again and again they climbed the snowy hill and again and again slid down the slope.

Late in the afternoon, Margaret sat down at the bottom of the hill to rest and to watch the approaching sunset. Father noticed that the sun was starting to sink behind the mountain and walked over to talk with her. "I think it's time for us to be starting home," he said.

"Oh, let me coast just one more time before we leave," begged Margaret.

"Let me coast once more, too," cried Roger.

"Roger can coast on my sled with me," said Margaret. "We can coast together."

"All right, just one more time," agreed Father. "By that time it will be almost dark and we must be on our way home. This coasting could go on forever, you know."

When they reached home, they took off their snow-covered coats and caps and shook them on the back porch. Next they sat around the fireplace to warm and dry themselves. "We had a great time coasting today, Mother," said Ruth. "You should have seen Roger steer the big sled down the hill. He steered it as well as Father could have done."

"I'm glad you had such a good time," said Mother. "Would you like some popcorn to eat while you are getting warm?"

"Oh, yes!" cried Margaret, running to get the wire popcorn popper. "Let me help you, Mother. It will be fun to hold the popper over the glowing coals in the fireplace. I like to watch the corn pop open."

Mother brought some corn to put in the wire corn popper. Then Margaret took hold of the long handle and held the popper over the hot coals. "Shake it gently to keep the corn moving, so it won't burn," said Mother.

Soon crackling sounds could be heard in the popper and white chunks of popcorn flew in all directions. In a few minutes the popper was completely filled with popped corn. Roger laughed as he watched the kernels explode in the popper. "They go every which way," he said gleefully.

Mother brought a couple of heavy hot pads to open the corn popper. Deftly she poured the popcorn into bowls, one for each member of the family. Then she poured melted butter over the popcorn in each bowl and gently sprinkled a little salt over the top.

The children's mouths watered as they watched their mother. The popcorn looked so good that they could hardly wait to begin eating it. Moments later they felt warm and comfortable as they sat around the fireplace, munching popcorn from their bowls. "What a perfect way to end a wonderful day of coasting," said Margaret.

"Yes," agreed Father. "Mother has chosen just the right thing for us. Eating this hot popcorn will make us feel warm and comfortable after we go to bed."

Playing
Basketball

During the noon hour each day in winter the children played outdoors at school. One day they asked Miss Rugen whether they could go to skate on Lily Pond. "No, there won't be time for you to go that far within an hour to skate," replied Miss Rugen.

"I wish our gymnasium was fixed up so we could play basketball," said Joey. "I have a basketball at home but all I can do is bounce it around."

"Well, you have a good idea," said Miss Rugen. "Maybe we can get the Board of Education to put up some backstops and baskets in

76

the gymnasium. Then you can organize some teams here in the room to play one another."

"That's wonderful!" cried Margaret. "Maybe we can organize both a boy's team and a girl's team right here in our room."

That evening when Margaret was helping Mother with the dishes she told her about their plans to play basketball at school. She explained that Miss Rugen was going to try to get the Board of Education to put up backstops and baskets in the gymnasium. "That's fine," said Mother. "Maybe our Parent Teacher Association can help in some way."

Each day at school from now on the pupils talked about their plans to play basketball. Margaret and the other girls who were interested in forming a girls' team gathered at Miss Rugen's desk. "What kind of uniforms will we need for our team?" they asked.

Miss Rugen smiled. " You'll need regular gym

suits," she replied, "and I think I can get enough suits for your team."

"Oh, good!" cried the girls. "Now we won't have to worry about our uniforms."

That afternoon Margaret was so excited that she could scarcely keep her mind on her lessons. She opened her arithmetic book to work the problems which Miss Rugen had assigned. She got out a sheet of paper and wrote her name at the top. Then she started to work the first problem, but her mind soon drifted off to playing basketball. Suddenly she realized that she would have to settle down to work in order to get all the problems done before class time.

During the afternoon recess the girls talked again about plans for their basketball team. "How can we get a basketball to start practicing?" asked Helen.

"We'll probably have to buy one," said Charlotte. "I wonder how much a ball will cost."

Joey, who was standing nearby, overheard the girls talking. "Remember, I have a basketball at home," he said.

"Do you want to sell it?" asked Margaret.

"No, but I might consider renting it," he answered in a helpful tone of voice.

Margaret thought for a moment and decided it might be a good idea to rent Joey's ball until they could get one of their own. "How much rent would you charge us?" she asked.

Joey hesitated and finally said, "Well, I'll rent it to you for a dollar."

"Bring it tomorrow so we can start practicing," cried the girls joyfully.

Joey brought the basketball to school and the girls took it out onto the school yard. They had a good time tossing it back and forth to one another, but it seemed a little heavy to them. Margaret tried to bounce it on the ground but it would hardly bounce at all.

The girls took the basketball into the classroom to show it to Miss Rugen. She looked at
it carefully and bounced it on the floor, but it
was sluggish in coming back to her hands.

"This is not a very good basketball," she said, "but you can probably use it for practicing until you can get another one."

Within a few days workmen came to put up backstops and baskets in the gymnasium. Miss Rugen announced that the gymnasium was ready for the children to use. "The boys and girls will have to take turns in using it," she said. "The boys can practice one day and the girls the next day."

The girls started practicing with Joey's heavy, sluggish basketball. They could throw the ball to one another but had trouble tossing it through the basket. Nearly every time they tried to make a basket, it hit the hoop and rolled off to one side.

The next morning as Margaret was leaving for school, her mother said, "You may find a surprise at school today."

Margaret turned to look at her mother.

"What kind of a surprise?" she asked. "Will it be something just for me or for the other children, too? Will it be something I will like?"

"Yes, it will be something you'll like, but I won't tell you more," Mother replied.

Margaret ran down the street to walk to school with Charlotte. "Mother said that I can look forward to a surprise at school today," she said excitedly, "but I can't guess what it will be. She wouldn't give me any clues."

"Do you think it will be something good or something bad?" asked Charlotte.

"It's supposed to be good," said Margaret. "That's the one thing Mother told me."

The two girls walked into their classroom, hung up their coats in the cloakroom, and took their seats with the other pupils. When school started Miss Rugen stood at her desk and said, "Good morning, girls and boys. I have a very happy surprise for you this morning. The Parent Teacher Association has presented us with a brand-new basketball."

All the children happily clapped their hands. They gazed at the new basketball Miss Rugen held in her hands. "So this is the surprise Mother told me about," Margaret thought.

The boys and girls took turns playing on alternate days with the new basketball. Day after day, first one team and then the other practiced hard in the gymnasium. Finally the girls challenged the boys to play a real basketball game. Miss Rugen offered to serve as referee. Both sides played hard, but the girls won. Margaret was never happier in her life.

The children kept on playing basketball until warm spring days arrived. One spring day Miss Rugen went to the window and noticed that the caterpillar was stirring in its box. "Come to watch," she called to her pupils. "The caterpillar is starting to change."

All the girls and boys gathered around to watch, but some of them couldn't see. "You'll have to take turns," said Miss Rugen. "Come up in groups of three or four to look."

The children now came up in groups of three or four to watch the caterpillar. "Oh, look!" cried one of them. "It is spinning a cocoon."

The little woolly caterpillar which had been curled fast asleep in its box all winter had now awakened in the warmth of spring. It was starting to spin a cocoon out of silken thread which its body made for the purpose. Soon its cocoon would look like a tiny felt sack attached to the twig in the box.

Each day the girls and boys watched the new cocoon in the box. Day after day it rested quietly on its slender twig. Finally one day Margaret noticed that it moved a little. "Come quick to see," she called. "The cocoon is getting ready to split."

Miss Rugen picked up the box from the window sill and carried it to her desk. She wanted all the children to be able to see what was about to happen. The boys and girls were speechless as they stood watching a damp, velvety moth struggle from its dry, felt-like cocoon. Soon the tawny yellow moth spread its wings as if to test them. "Oh, how beautiful it is with black dots on its yellow wings!" cried Helen. "What kind of butterfly is it?"

"It isn't a butterfly at all," replied Miss Rugen. "It's a moth, which we commonly call a tiger moth."

Briefly she explained the difference between butterflies and moths to the children. Then she turned to Margaret and said, "Since you brought the caterpillar to school, would you like to take the moth outside to set it free?"

"Oh, yes," answered Margaret eagerly.

Carefully she cupped her hands around the

little moth to carry it outside. Charlotte and Helen walked along with her out of the building. As she walked she could feel the little moth fluttering in her hands. "Now let it loose," cried Helen eagerly.

Margaret looked about at the sunny, open playground. "No, not here," she said. "I think I should wait to turn it loose where there are some trees and bushes."

The girls walked slowly on down the street, and Margaret kept looking for a good place to turn the moth loose.

"Let it go," cried the girls. "Why carry it any farther?"

Margaret completely ignored the girls and kept on looking. Soon she came to a vacant lot where there were bushes and trees. Suddenly she held her arms outstretched and slowly opened her hands to form a platform for the moth. For a brief moment the moth poised on her fingertips and waved its tawny wings. Then with a flutter it took off for the nearby bushes.

Margaret waved to it as if she were waving good-bye to a friend. The girls now walked back to school and told Miss Rugen about releasing the moth. "Margaret merely opened her hands and away it flew to a bush," said Helen.

"That shows where moths really belong," said Miss Rugen. "They thrive in the woods, where they can flutter from branch to branch in the nearby bushes and trees."

Winning a Prize
as a Sophomore

MARGARET was very active and happy during her last year in the elementary school. She worked hard on her studies in order to get ready for high school the following year. She was one of the leading players on the girls' basketball team which had a very successful year. They played many games during the winter season and nearly always won.

One day in early spring when Margaret was returning home from school, she noticed her father's automobile parked on the street in front of their home. Her father was walking from the house toward the automobile carrying a stack of his drawings. At once she knew that he was going to a factory and wanted to go with him. "Oh, Father," she called, starting to run, "may I go along with you today?"

Often Father took her with him when he went places to help set up new printing presses which he had designed. When Margaret reached the automobile, she held the door open while Father put his drawings inside. Once more she asked, "May I go with you?"

"No, not today," replied Father, "but I have a surprise for you. Next Saturday I'll take you with me on a trip to a foundry at Dunellen. That's the foundry that makes the beds for new printing presses which I design."

"How wonderful!" exclaimed Margaret. "Of course I want to go with you to Dunellen. I've never visited a foundry before."

From then on she could hardly wait for Saturday to come. Early Saturday morning she and Father climbed into the family automobile and took off for Dunellen. Along the way she talked with him about the sights beside the road, such as farm houses, animals, and trees. At other times she talked about school, basketball, and her pets. Father nodded as if listening but was too busy thinking to answer her.

The foundry was a dark, dingy brick building with several tall smokestacks. Black smoke rolled out of the smokestacks, clouding the atmosphere. The air about the building was filled with the acrid odor of hot metal.

When Margaret and Father reached the foundry Father led the way into a small office. Then a plant manager took them up a narrow, cement stairway to a dark, dirty platform, surrounded by a soot-covered railing. From there they could look down and see men working at furnaces on the floor of the foundry. "Don't lean over too far," cautioned the plant manager.

"I won't," replied Margaret, "but I want to see as much as possible."

From the platform she could see workmen in dirty, grimy overalls moving here and there. In the dimness she could see mysterious forms, including hoists and a variety of metal containers. Little cars ran along tracks to carry loads from one place to another.

A short distance from where Margaret stood there was a huge furnace. Through cracks around the edges of the furnace door she could see orange-colored flames inside like those in a heating stove. Beside the furnace stood a man with a long pole in his hands, somewhat like a poker. On his head he wore a helmet-like hat with a visor which he could pull down.

Soon someone gave a muffled command, "Pour iron!" Promptly the man opened the furnace door and bubbling red-hot metal came pouring out into a huge container.

Margaret was thrilled with joyous surprise. She had never seen a more beautiful sight in her life. She was delighted at the spectacular beauty of the molten-hot metal gurgling and giving forth reddish-gold sparks as it splashed into the container. She never forgot the beauty of this wondrous scene. Years later, after she became a photographer, she made a special photograph of this scene for others to enjoy.

After Margaret finished the elementary school, she had to attend high school in nearby Plainfield, because there was no high school in Bound Brook. Each day she and some of her friends rode a commuter train to and from Plainfield. On the first day her cheeks flushed with excitement as she swung up the steps of the train with a stack of books under her arm. Then she hurried down the aisle to find a seat followed by Helen, Charlotte, and several other close friends on their way to school.

High school opened up many new opportunities for Margaret. She made new friends readily and took part in numerous high school activities. She was chosen to help edit the high school paper and to serve as YWCA Club representative at a regional conference.

Her second year of high school was even more exciting than her first year. One day Miss Evans, the sophomore English teacher, announced a contest for excellence in story writing. She explained that the contest would be open to all high school students.

The students in the sophomore English class listened closely as Miss Evans spoke. "Of course, a senior student and occasionally a junior student usually wins this contest," she stated. Then she added, "Even though a sophomore has little chance of winning, if any of you want to enter the contest, you will be excused from taking regular English examinations."

One of the boys raised his hand to ask a question. "Will the person who wins the contest get any kind of prize?"

"Yes," replied Miss Evans. "The prize will be fifteen dollars worth of books."

"How long must the story be?" asked one of the girls in the class.

"It must contain eight hundred words, neatly handwritten," replied Miss Evans.

Margaret promptly decided to enter the contest. She had little hope of winning but thought it would be exciting to take part. She told Miss Evans and was excused from taking the regular English examinations.

Through the coming months she became so busy with other school activities that she put off writing the story. She worked out a good theme in her mind but failed to put it down on paper. Finally one day near the end of the school year Miss Evans suddenly announced,

"Those of you who have entered the English contest must turn in your stories today."

Margaret had a frightful feeling of panic following this announcement. She trembled as she picked up her books to walk out of the classroom. As she neared the door, Miss Evans made a further anouncement. "If any of you need more time to finish your story, you may take it directly to the principal at his home no later than 5:30 this evening."

Margaret walked from the classroom in deep thought. She decided that she would still try to write the story. The minute school was out she would go to the library to start writing and would try to have her story finished by 5:30 as Miss Evans had ordered.

At three o'clock when the school day ended Margaret headed for the library, followed by her friend Helen, who was eager to help her in any way she could. She sat down in a quiet corner and started to write. She wrote faster and faster as she thought through the story. Her story was about a boy who wanted a dog. In the beginning the boy found a dog that he liked very much but lost it.

Helen sat beside Margaret and counted the words that she wrote. After Margaret had written for a while Helen looked up at the clock. "It's four-thirty," she said, "and you have written six hundred and eighty words. You need one hundred and twenty words more and have only an hour left in which to finish your story and deliver it to the principal's house."

Margaret nodded and started to write faster than ever. She ended the story by telling how the boy found the dog again. It was now five-twenty, and she had just time enough left to run to the principal's home.

On the next to the last day of school Miss Evans told Margaret that the principal wanted to see her in his office. Margaret's heart pounded as she hurried down the hall, but she found a happy surprise awaiting her. "Come in, come in," called the principal when she reached the open door of his office. He stretched out his hand and added, "Congratulations. You have won the contest for writing the best story. This is the first time a sophomore has ever won. Your prize will be fifteen dollars in books of your choice. Tell Miss Evans what books you would like."

The principal explained that the books would be presented to her during the commencement exercises. At once she hurried back to her room to talk with Miss Evans. She told her what the principal had said, and what three books she wanted as prizes. Then Miss Evans agreed to have the books ready and neatly wrapped for the principal to give her.

After school she rushed home to break the

good news to her mother. On commencement night she put on a pretty white dress and placed a big white bow in her hair. Then proudly she joined the crowd in the gymnasium.

The platform in the gymnasium was decorated with green palms. The principal and other speakers, looking very dignified and serious, sat in a row on the platform. Soon the principal started to make the awards and called out in a deep, solemn voice, "For excellence in literary composition, Margaret White."

Margaret proudly walked up the aisle to the platform where the principal was waiting. He leaned forward to present her with a package of books, decorated with a huge white ribbon bow on top. As she turned from accepting the package, she was greeted by loud and warm applause from the audience.

Later in the exercises the seniors walked up to the platform one by one to receive their diplomas. After the ceremonies were over, the chairs were folded and stacked against the wall to make room for the graduation dance. The orchestra began to play and couples started to glide out on the floor and dance to the rhythm of the music. Soon the dance floor was almost completely filled.

Margaret watched dancers joyfully from the sidelines. This was one of the greatest evenings in her life. Her only disappointment was that no boy asked her to dance.

Early Steps in Photography

DURING MARGARET's last year in high school she suffered deep sorrow. Her father, whom she greatly loved and admired, became ill and died. The White family home was filled with intense grief and concern.

Following Father's death, Mother sat down at the dining room table with her three children, Ruth, Margaret, and Roger, to make plans for the future. "We'll have to spend our money very carefully from now on," she said.

"Maybe I can get a job to help pay expenses," said Margaret in a serious tone of voice.

"No, that won't be necessary," replied

Mother, shaking her head. "You must go on to college to continue your education."

"How can I go to college if we have to be careful about money?" asked Margaret.

"We'll find a way," said Mother. "That's the reason we are talking things over."

"Well, I can go to Teachers College at Columbia University in New York," Margaret suggested. "Then I can live at home and go back and forth with some of my friends every day. That will cost much less than living at a college away from home."

Mother approved and the following fall Margaret enrolled as a freshman at Teachers College. She left home about seven o'clock in the morning and sometimes didn't get home until ten-thirty at night. She started to specialize in biology and zoology to learn as much about wild life in nature as possible. Someday she hoped to become an expert on wild life and be sent on expeditions to different parts of the world. She even dreamed of going on safaris to Africa to look for rare specimens of animal life.

Sometimes as she rode the train she wondered how she could earn money to do all the things that she wanted to do later in life. One day she happened to think that she could earn money by becoming a photographer. She could pay her way by taking pictures wherever she went, even to distant parts of the world. At Columbia University she signed up to take a course in photography and her mother purchased her a second-hand camera to get started.

Near the end of the school year, Margaret began to look for a job for the summer. One late spring day between classes she went to the student personnel office to seek help in getting a job. Outside the entrance she paused to read job announcements which were listed on a large bulletin board. There she came across another girl who was also looking for a summer job. "My name is Madge Goldstein," she said. "Are you looking for a summer job?"

"Yes, I'm Margaret White and I have to work this summer," replied Margaret.

Together the girls found an announcement of an opening for a camp counselor with knowledge of photography, also for two other counselors. "Oh, look!" cried Margaret. "That opening for a counselor with a knowledge of photography sounds good to me."

"Well, I don't know anything about photography, but I would like to get one of those other counselor jobs," said Madge.

The announcement explained that the counselors would work at Camp Agaming, Lake Bantam, Connecticut. "What a thrilling place to spend a summer!" exclaimed Margaret.

The girls went into the student personnel office and filed applications to become counselors at Camp Agaming. Within a few days they were overjoyed to receive letters saying that they had been employed as counselors for the summer. Margaret almost cried with joy as she read her letter to her mother.

On their first night at Camp Agaming the counselors held a meeting with the camp directors, Mr. and Mrs. Rohrig, on the shores of Lake Bantam. They made plans for the summer and talked and laughed together. Margaret felt happy to join such an agreeable group in such beautiful surroundings.

One evening after supper in the dining room when the children were restless and noisy, Margaret hopped up on a bench and called out, "Would you like to hear a true story about a beautiful butterfly?"

"Yes, yes," cried the boys and girls. "Tell us about the butterfly."

Happily Margaret reached deep into her

pocket and pulled out a black swallowtail butterfly chrysalis. She held up this dry, yellow-brown chrysalis so that everybody could see it. She explained how a green caterpillar, with black stripes, sheds its last skin and goes to sleep in a chrysalis. Then she said, "When the sleeping creature in the chrysalis finally wakes up it comes forth in the form of a beautiful swallowtail butterfly."

All the boys and girls gathered around Margaret to look at the chrysalis. They asked question after question about it. Some even wanted to hold it in their hands.

Margaret was delighted to find them so interested. From then on she helped them to recognize strange flowers which they brought from the woods. One day she found two garter snakes which she brought to show them. The children were wide-eyed with surprise. "Aren't they dangerous?" asked a girl.

"No, they are perfectly harmless," replied Margaret as she held the snakes higher for her to see. "You need to learn much about snakes so that you can tell which ones are harmless and which ones are dangerous. These are garter snakes, and garter snakes are harmless."

"What do snakes eat?" asked one of the boys curiously.

"Small snakes like these eat earthworms and larger snakes eat toads and frogs," explained Margaret.

"May we keep these snakes for pets?" asked an older girl.

"Yes, but you'll need to keep them in a cage or they will slither away," she said.

She sent one of the boys to ask Mr. Rohrig for a suitable cage for the snakes. When he came back with a cage, she held the snakes close to the cage door and they crawled inside. Then all the children crowded around closely to watch them and decided that they should have names. After considering many names, they chose to call the larger snake "Icky Phooie" and the smaller one "Icky Goo."

Every day from then on the children collected earthworms to feed the snakes. Soon they discovered that Icky Phooie, the larger snake, would come to the cage door when they came to feed it. Then it would eagerly take worms from their hands for its dinner.

That night when all the children had gone to bed Margaret wrote these lines in her diary:

"It is such a lot of fun thinking up catchy ways to tell the youngsters about nature. I try to make it interesting by telling them a legend or a superstition that is attached to each flower. I am considered the ultimate authority on everything in the land, sea, and sky and am expected to account for the wiggle of every antenna, the intent and purpose of every bug, and the twinkle of every star.

It's funny and wonderful the way the children bring me every bug and flower as though they were making me costly gifts."

About halfway through the camping period Mr. and Mrs. Rohrig arranged a three-day hike up Mount Tom, the highest mountain in Connecticut. They planned this trip for themselves and some of the counselors and children in the camp. Margaret found the mountain trails so beautiful that she made a second trip to take photographs. Also she took photographs of Lake Bantam and the camp.

When Mr. and Mrs. Rohrig saw Margaret's photographs, they were fascinated with them. They liked them so well that they asked her whether she could make picture postcards from them. This question caused her to beam with joy. "Of course I can," she replied.

Mr. and Mrs. Rohrig picked out the photographs they liked best and gave her an order to

print five hundred postcards from them. She had already set up a darkroom at camp to show the children how to develop photographic film. From then on she spent night after night in the darkroom printing the pictures on postcards. Her friend Madge constantly helped her.

One night as they hung postcards about the darkroom to dry, Madge looked at her watch and said, "It's nearly one o'clock in the morning. Let's quit for tonight."

"Not yet," replied Margaret, looking at the stack of cards still to be printed. "Mr. Rohrig wants me to deliver all the cards by tomorrow morning. Some of the parents will come after their children tomorrow and they may wish to purchase postcards to take home with them."

Margaret's picture postcards proved to be very popular with the parents. Within a few days Mr. and Mrs. Rohrig sold nearly three hundred of them to parents who came to the camp. Then they ordered five hundred more postcards from her to be delivered later.

Margaret did so well selling postcards at the camp that she decided to try to sell them to merchants in town who sold things to tourists. She selected some of her best pictures of Mount Tom and Lake Bantam to take along as samples. Nervously she put them in a large manila envelope to carry under her arm.

Her first stop was at a drug store. With her heart pounding, she marched back to a counter and carefully laid out her samples before the manager. He looked at the pictures and frowned. "No, we aren't interested," he said. "We sell less expensive cards."

Margaret felt a bit downhearted as she left the drug store. From there she stepped into a gift shop next door. Much to her surprise the owner wouldn't even look at her samples. "We have all the postcards we need," he said.

By now Margaret was almost ready to give up, but she took a deep breath and entered the Laircourt Gift Shop. This shop had an air of elegance and refinement about it. Promptly a lovely, white-haired lady, Mrs. Adams, one of the owners, came forward and asked graciously, "May I help you, please?"

Margaret explained that she was a photographer and that she would like to show her samples of some of her postcards. "Of course," replied Mrs. Adams, "but let me call my sister, who is my partner, to help look at them."

The two white-haired ladies were delighted with Margaret's samples. "Your pictures are charming and we'll order some of them," said Mrs. Adams. Her sister agreed.

The sisters treated Margaret as if she were an expert photographer and took her outside to look at their garden. There they pointed out the quaint sloping roof lines of the Lodge and the antique lantern hanging over the door. "Will you take some pictures of our garden?"

"Yes, indeed," cried Margaret. "This is an excellent spot for taking pictures. We can get some beautiful effects here."

The ladies smiled pleasantly and ordered five hundred picture postcards of their garden. Margaret felt so happy about this successful visit that she almost danced down the street. When she reached the dining room at the camp supper was already over, but she didn't care. With orders she had obtained in town and her camp orders, she now had to make over a thousand picture postcards before leaving for home. She ordered a supply of postcard picture paper and planned to spend all her time in the darkroom. She hired two boys to help her.

Part of the paper which she ordered arrived and she and the two boys set up a production line to print the postcards. Each day they

114

worked from early in the morning until late in the evening. The two boys were fascinated by the way the films and chemicals printed beautiful pictures on the postcards. Margaret told them interesting stories as they worked to help make the time pass faster.

All went well until Margaret ran out of blank paper, and she still had two hundred and fifty postcards left to print. The remainder of her order for the paper failed to arrive until the evening before she was to leave for home. Now she was frantic, wondering what to do.

At last she decided to stay up all night and try to finish the postcards before she had to leave. A young boy from the town offered to help her, but he had never worked in a darkroom before. Luckily, he caught on quickly and the two of them worked well together. They managed to finish the postcards only a few hours before Margaret's train would leave.

Mr. Rohrig offered to take her to the railroad station. He looked at her finished postcards and said, "Your picture postcards are outstanding. The parents and everybody else liked them very much."

When Margaret boarded the train she was so tired that she could scarcely walk to her seat. Even though she was exhausted, she felt a magical glow of happiness inside her. She had had a wonderful summer and with it all had discovered her special talents as a photographer. Also she had the deep satisfaction of knowing that she had undertaken a difficult task and had done it well.

Choosing
a Life Career

WHEN MARGARET returned home from Camp Agaming she wasn't sure whether or not she would get to return to college that fall. She counted the money which she had earned from working as a counselor and from selling picture postcards. Although she had saved every penny, she still lacked enough to pay her way.

Fortunately her mother had some good news for her. She told her that a Mr. Munger and his sister wanted to talk with her. She wondered whether this had anything to do with her college education, but her mother couldn't give her any further information about the matter.

Without wasting any time Margaret put on her best dress and hurried to the address which her mother had given her. She felt uneasy as she walked up to the door of a large, white house. She rang the bell and a small gray-haired man answered the door. "I'm Margaret White," she said to introduce herself.

"Come in, Margaret," said Mr. Munger graciously. "My sister and I have been looking forward to meeting you."

He led the way into a well-furnished parlor, where a charming white-faced lady sat at a tea table. "Would you care for a cup of tea, my dear?" asked Miss Munger softly.

"Yes, thank you," answered Margaret, nervously seating herself in a chair.

"We won't keep you in suspense, Margaret," said Mr. Munger. "My sister and I have founded an Education Aid Association to help worthy college students. You have been recommended to us as a good student who will benefit from help in continuing your education."

"Oh, thank you!" exclaimed Margaret. "I'll appreciate anything you can do for me."

She was so excited by this surprise that she ran all the way home to break the good news to her mother. She flung open the door and shouted, "Mother, I am going to get to go to college this fall after all!"

Margaret explained to her mother that she and other good students had been recommended for scholarships by some of their high school teachers. This year she would attend the University of Michigan. "Now I can hardly wait to get started," she said.

"Congratulations, Margaret," said Mother. "You're a very deserving girl and I'm glad that others feel the same way."

During the next few days Margaret swirled around in a cloud of happiness as she unpacked her camp things and repacked her clothes and books for college. When she reached the campus at Ann Arbor, she felt as if she was in a dream world. After she checked in at her rooming house, she took a walk.

It was late afternoon and dusk was falling around the big shadowy buildings. Here and there students were standing in groups talking and laughing. As Margaret sauntered about she liked the feeling of belonging here.

She signed up for several science courses, including herpetology, the study of reptiles. Also she kept looking for ways to keep on with her photography. Soon she met the editor of the college yearbook, who invited her to take photographs for the book. One day he asked, "Would you like to take some artistic photographs of the engineering building from unusual angles?" He hesitated a moment and then added, "No, you couldn't take them."

"Why couldn't I?" asked Margaret.

"Because you would have to climb up onto the roof of the building with your camera," replied the editor.

Margaret hooted at this statement. "I wouldn't be afraid to climb up onto the roof of the building," she said. "I'll climb anywhere to take a good photograph."

The editor shrugged his shoulders. "All right, then, if you want to try," he said.

On Saturday morning Margaret gathered up her camera and went to take the picture. Holding tightly to the bulky camera, she climbed out of an upstairs window onto a sloping roof. Then with the help of a rope, she crawled to the peak of the roof and slid down the other side. There she propped her camera into position and sighted to take the photographs she wanted to obtain. All the while her heart pounded with excitement.

A few days later the editor reported that her photographs were just what he needed. He invited her to dinner at the University Union Building. From then on she enjoyed many social affairs at the University.

One day she met a graduate student who was completing work for his doctor's degree in engineering. Soon she and this graduate student, whom everyone called Chappie, fell in love.

Shortly after the school year ended Margaret and Chappie were married. Following his graduation Chappie obtained a position on the faculty at Purdue University at Lafayette, Indiana. Then Margaret enrolled as a student at Purdue University to continue her education.

When they were married Chappie made Margaret's wedding ring himself out of a gold nugget. While tapping the ring into shape with a miniature hammer, he accidentally broke it.

At first Margaret and Chappie were very

happy, but they had different interests in life. At Purdue University he was so enthusiastic about his engineering work that it was hard for him to become interested in Margaret's worms, snakes, and bugs. All the while Margaret felt like a student rather than the wife of a faculty member. Thus, after two years, their marriage, like their wedding ring, was broken.

At this time Margaret needed one more year to complete her college education. For this last year she decided to attend Cornell University at Ithaca, New York. There she would be able to take several science courses that she wanted as part of her college education.

When she reached Ithaca she looked about for a job to help pay her expenses. At first she applied for a position as a waitress in a restaurant. The manager asked her whether she had any experience as a waitress. In reply she explained that she had never been a waitress but that once she had been a counselor in a children's camp. "Well, that wasn't the right kind of experience you will need here," he said.

Slowly she walked from the restaurant back to the college campus. On the way she decided to apply for a position in the college library. Inside she walked up to a librarian seated at a counter and said, "I would like to apply for some kind of job here."

The librarian looked at her and shook her head. "I'm sorry, but all our library jobs have been filled," she said.

Margaret's shoulders drooped with discouragement. With heavy steps she walked back to the dormitory room and flung herself wearily on the bed. She knew that she had to earn money to spend this year in college. Tears started to roll down her cheeks as she wondered what she could do to earn a living.

Suddenly through her tears she happened to

glance at her old camera standing on her desk. The sight of this camera gave her an idea. She recalled how once she had taken photographs at camp with this camera and sold them. She decided to try her luck at photography again.

Quickly she dried her tears, picked up her camera, and hurried out onto the campus. She started to look around for beautiful scenes to photograph, including the old, ivy-covered buildings and the nearby waterfalls above Cayuga Lake. She felt certain that students would buy photographs of these scenes.

From then on she spent all of her spare time taking photographs. Finally from her collection of photographs she selected ten which would make the best ones to sell. She made arrangements to use the darkroom of a commercial photographer for making more prints. There she worked night after night to get a soft effect to make her photographs look like paintings.

At last, just before Christmas, she had finished enough photographs to try selling them. She set up a sales stand in the corridor just outside the dining room. Uneasily she arranged the photographs and propped some of them up

on the table to make them look attractive. Then she stepped back a short distance from the table to see how they looked.

Soon, much to her delight, students crowded around the table to look at her photographs. They were fascinated with them and examined them one by one. They bought some of them for Christmas gifts and for their rooms. They bought some of them for their parents, their boy friends, and their girl friends.

Margaret's photographs sold so well that she hired other students to help her sell them. She even arranged for the college book store to sell them. From this beginning her fame spread and she was invited to take photographs for the cover of the Alumni News.

Soon she began to get letters from persons who admired her photographs. Some, who especially liked her photographs of buildings on the campus, suggested that she take up architectural photography. She showed one of these letters to a close girl friend in the dormitory. "How exciting!" exclaimed her friend. "Why not become an architectural photographer?"

Margaret shook her head. "This suggestion comes to me too late," she said. "Within a few months I'll be graduating from college with a major in biology. Besides, even though I'm a photographer, I know little or nothing about architectural photography."

Her friend wasn't ready to forget the idea. "Why don't you talk it over with an architect?" she said. "You could take along a collection of your photographs of buildings to show him what you can do."

Margaret decided that this might be a good suggestion. She already was planning to go to New York during the spring vacation to look for a job at the Museum of Natural History. While there she could take time to look up an architect in the city and show him some of her photographs, as her friend had suggested.

When she arrived in New York she inquired at the museum for the name of a prominent architect. "One of the best is Mr. Benjamin Moskowitz of the architectural firm of York and Sawyer," was the response.

Carefully Margaret got her photographs together, hoping to show them to Mr. Moskowitz. She arranged them neatly in a portfolio and placed it on a table. Then she put on her new crepe dress with the pleated skirt. Finally she pulled on her blue hat, which exactly matched her dress, and looked at herself in a mirror.

It was late in the afternoon before she located the architectural firm. She stepped into a large reception room and asked to see Mr. Moskowitz. Just at that moment, a tall man in an obvious hurry walked past her. The receptionist looked up, nodded her head toward the man, and said, "That's Mr. Moskowitz over there. He is already starting home for the day."

Quickly Margaret turned and followed Mr. Moskowitz to the elevator. She introduced herself and tried to tell him what she wanted, but he kept on walking. When they came to the elevator door Margaret reached into her portfolio and pulled out a photograph to show him. Casually he glanced at it, then looked at it intently. "Did you take this?" he asked.

"Yes," replied Margaret. She explained that she wanted to talk with him about becoming an architectural photographer.

"Have you any other photographs with you?" he asked earnestly.

Margaret nodded her head and pulled the rest of the photographs from her portfolio. Mr. Moskowitz glanced at them and said, "Good! Let's go back to my office so I can look at them."

When they reached Mr. Moskowitz's office, he stood the pictures up against a wall. Without saying a word he stepped over to his telephone, called several other architects in the company, and said, "Come to my office. I have something interesting to show you."

Soon the room was filled with architects looking admiringly at Margaret's collection of photographs. They asked her all sorts of questions about her techniques of taking and finishing photographs. She answered all their questions very carefully and asked them many thoughtful questions in return.

Even though it was time for the architects to go home, they stayed around for over an hour to talk with her. One after another they complimented her on both her knowledge of photography and her fine photographic ability. All agreed that she could readily become a real success as an architectural photographer.

Photographs
in a Steel Mill

WHEN MARGARET graduated from Cornell University she decided to set up a photographic studio in Cleveland, Ohio. She rode a train to Buffalo and took a night boat on Lake Erie the rest of the way. The early morning foggy air wrapped around her and clung to her hair as she stood watching for a glimpse of the city.

As the night boat plowed through the waves of the lake, the eastern sky slowly brightened with the rising sun. Suddenly, as if by magic, the skyline of Cleveland appeared. Margaret shivered with delight as the shadowy buildings seemed to loom up from the lake. Right now she felt as if she were standing on the doorstep of a bright future career.

In Cleveland she rented a small apartment to serve as her home and studio. She decided to use her full name, Margaret Bourke-White, with a hyphen between Bourke and White. She knew this would be pleasing to her mother because Bourke had been her mother's family name. Later many people called her Peggy.

Her apartment was very small. She used her kitchen sink for both developing her film and washing her prints. She had only one good gray suit, which she wore either with a red hat and gloves or a blue hat and gloves.

Once she was settled she started to call on architects and obtained an assignment to photograph a new school building. This building had just been finished and stood in a muddy field. There were still piles of gravel and building scraps all over the yard.

On her first trip to the school Margaret walked through the mud to look at the building from all angles. She decided that the good architectural lines of the building would show up best against a lovely sunset. When she tried to take the picture, however, she discovered that the sun set on the back side of the building. Then she realized that she would have to take the photograph with the helpful light of a rising sun rather than a setting sun.

The next morning she set her alarm clock to awaken her before sunrise. Then, carrying her camera equipment, she trudged through the dark streets to the school building. She set up her equipment and waited for the sun to come up. Unfortunately, she couldn't carry out her plans because clouds moved in and hid the morning sun. For four mornings in a row she rushed to the school building but couldn't take any photographs because of clouds in the sky.

On the fifth morning she found the sunrise perfect. She set up her camera before the building, but everywhere the view was spoiled by piles of rubbish. Finally she decided to try some simple landscaping to hide part of the background. She ran to a nearby florist and bought an armload of flowers. Then she stuck them in a neat row in the muddy ground.

When she had everything ready she placed her camera low so she could shoot through the tops of the flowers. From here, she took a few shots of the building and then moved the flowers to take other shots. She kept moving about until she had taken photographs of all the good angles of the building. By now the sun was high in the sky.

The architects were highly pleased with Margaret's photographs. They were amazed to find beautiful flowers planted around their school building and loudly praised her for her talent.

Her photographs were published in *Architecture* magazine, and the Bourke-White Studio enjoyed its first success.

Later Margaret walked to different parts of the city to solicit photographic work from architects and landscapers. One day she happened to pass a park where a preacher stood on a soapbox preaching a sermon. She was fascinated because there were no listeners, but he was completely surrounded by pigeons. At once she wanted to take a picture of this scene, but knew that she wouldn't have time to run home to get her camera. Quickly she ran to a nearby camera shop and cried, "May I borrow a camera? There's a shot I just have to take."

The owner of the shop, Mr. Bemis, promptly loaded a camera and handed it to her. With the camera in her hands, she rushed back to the park and took a photograph of the preacher and the pigeons. She returned the camera, thanked

Mr. Bemis and told him about the photograph she had taken. He asked her many questions about her photographic work and she told him that somehow she hoped to get into steel mills to take photographs. "Ever since my father took me to visit an iron foundry in New Jersey I've wanted to take photographs inside a steel mill," she explained.

"Well, that's an unusual ambition for a woman photographer, but I hope you find a way to do it," he said.

Mr. Bemis proved to be a very helpful friend to Margaret. He had a good knowledge of the latest photographic materials and techniques. Often she went to him for advice.

Right now she was especially interested in an area along the waterfront called the Flats, where most of the steel mills were located. The smoke stacks rising from factories formed a picturesque background along Lake Erie. Switch engines clattered as they pushed and pulled coal cars here and there. The blasts of tugboat whistles kept sounding as tugboats shoved coal barges down the busy Cuyahoga River.

Whenever Margaret could spare time from taking pictures for her customers she went down to the Flats to take pictures on her own. Happily she took pictures of factories, smokestacks, bridges, and barges. She even took pictures of nearby mountains of iron ore and coal with the steel mills in the background.

Sometimes in the late evening, after it grew too dark to take photographs, she sat and watched the smoky, foggy steel mills from a distance. She enjoyed seeing the flashes of light that came from the factories and listening to the noisy clanging sounds of the machinery inside. Mostly she liked to watch the strings of little ladle cars, loaded with red-gold molten slag, come bustling out of the mills. Then she watched carefully as the cars, one by one, dumped the glowing metal, which rolled like hot candle drippings, down the mountain of slag.

Watching this drama of steel against the dark

night made Margaret all the more eager to photograph steel mills on the inside. Then, quite by chance, a chain of events gave her this opportunity to photograph the inside of a steel mill. She heard that the Union Trust Company, a bank, was interested in buying an industrial picture for the cover of its magazine, *Trade Winds*. Hurriedly she took her portfolio of pictures to the bank, and the man in charge selected her photograph of a high-level bridge. "That's a striking photograph," he said.

A short time later the Union Trust Company called Margaret and asked her to take a photograph of a prize-winning steer on exhibit in the lobby. When she saw the jet-black steer, surrounded by the white marble walls of the lobby she realized that she would have difficulty photographing him.

Somewhat baffled, she called on her friend, Mr. Bemis, for advice. "You'll need strong artificial light, since there are no windows to admit light in the lobby," he said.

"There are good electric lights in the lobby," said Margaret. "What do you mean by strong artificial lights?"

"I mean flash powder," answered Mr. Bemis. "Have you ever used any?"

Margaret shook her head. "No, I've never used any because I've never needed it in any photographic work before."

"Well, I'll lend you my apparatus, but I don't want you to blow your hands off," he said. "If you can wait until lunchtime, I'll send Earl from my shop over to help you use it."

Margaret agreed and during the noon hour Earl set off charges of powder while she took the pictures. The bank officials liked one of the photographs so well that they ordered 485 copies for customers and newspapers, to be delivered early the next morning.

Frantically she ran to Mr. Bemis's shop to tell him about the order. "How can I get 485 copies by tomorrow morning?" she asked.

"There's only one way," he replied. "We'll have to make them right here. There isn't a studio in the city that would make so many of them on such short notice."

That evening Mr. Bemis, Margaret, and Earl went to the darkroom to start to make copies of the photograph. They formed a production line and worked all night printing pictures of the prize-winning, black steer. The next morning Margaret delivered the photographs and afterwards went home to sleep. As she dozed off she thought, "I've made enough money on these photographs to buy a new lens for my camera, good for taking photographs in steel mills."

The next time Margaret saw Mr. Bemis she asked, "How am I ever going to get into the steel mills to take pictures?"

"Why not ask Mr. John Sherwin, president of the Union Trust Company, to introduce you to the president of the steel mill?" suggested Mr. Bemis, scratching his head.

"That's a good idea," said Margaret. "But he may never have heard of me. He may never have seen the picture of the black steer I took in the lobby of the bank."

"Well, I think it's worth giving a try," said Mr. Bemis.

When Margaret called on Mr. Sherwin he couldn't understand why she wanted to take photographs in a dirty steel mill. Even so, he gave her a letter of introduction to Elroy Kulas, president of the Otis Steel Company. "Thank you, Mr. Sherwin, for helping to make my photographic dreams come true," she said.

Immediately Margaret went to see Mr. Kulas. Her heart pounded as she stepped into his office. Nervously she told him why she was eager to take photographs of steelmaking. She explained that she wasn't trying to sell him anything but merely wanted to experiment.

"Why do you want to experiment in a hot, dirty steel mill?" asked Mr. Kulas.

"Because I think steel mills are beautiful," replied Margaret. "They haven't been designed for beauty, but they have hidden beauty because their lines are clear and simple."

Mr. Kulas shook his head. "There's another factor to consider, Margaret," he said. "Steel mills are very dangerous. The heat is overpowering and sparks are flying everywhere from the molten metal. Besides, the air is filled with the fumes of acid."

"I know, but I'm not afraid," said Margaret. "Just give me permission and I promise not to cause you any problems."

Mr. Kulas was pleased with her sincerity. He called in some of the steel mill officials and ordered them to allow her to take photographs in the plant. Then he turned to her and said, "I'm leaving on a five-month's trip to Europe. When I return, I'll want to see some of the photographs you take."

Margaret's first night at the steel mill was a thrilling experience. Happily she set up her cameras and started to shoot photographs. When the operator of the blast furnace shouted, "Make steel!" she fairly gasped with joy. She stared in amazement as she watched the glowing liquid steel gush out into the waiting ladle. She shot photographs as fast as she could, some showing sparks flying from the molten metal like sparklers on the Fourth of July.

She could hardly wait to develop the photographs, but she was doomed to unexpected disappointment. She couldn't see a trace of anything on the dull gray film.

Once more she consulted her friend, Mr.

Bemis. "The shots were wonderful and I can't understand what happened," she said.

"You didn't have enough light to get clear photographs," explained Mr. Bemis.

"Oh, no, the light was blinding," protested Margaret. "The whole plant was lit up from the glow of the red-hot steel."

"I know," said Mr. Bemis, "but molten steel gives off heat, not true light."

Again Mr. Bemis and his assistant Earl agreed to help Margaret. They set up floodlights and shot off flash powder while she handled the camera. Unfortunately, these artificial lights proved to be too weak for her to obtain good photographs. "What shall I do now?" she asked Mr. Bemis. "Do you know of anyone who has taken good photographs in a steel mill? Maybe I can talk with him."

"No, but I have another suggestion," said Mr. Bemis. "I know of a salesman who has some new photographic flares which are brighter than any other lighting device ever used before. He happens to be in the city and I'll bring him to the steel mill tonight with some of his flares."

"How wonderful!" cried Margaret. "I certainly hope they will work."

That night Mr. Bemis and the salesman met Margaret at the steel mill with the flares. Then Mr. Bemis stood on one side of her and the salesman on the other, each holding a flare in his hand. In taking shots with her camera, she had to work fast because the flares lasted for only thirty seconds.

The next night they developed the films, eager to find out what the photographs would be like. They shouted with glee when the negatives turned out to be almost perfect. At last, after nearly five months, Margaret had achieved her goal.

Despite this achievement Margaret faced still

another problem. She couldn't find paper sensitive enough for enlarging and printing the photographs. Finally Mr. Bemis helped her to obtain some photographic paper which was imported from Belgium, and her last problem was finally solved.

A few days later Mr. Kulas, president of Otis Steel Company, returned from his trip to Europe. On his first day back in his office, he inquired about Margaret's photographs. When told how clear and beautiful they were, he expressed a desire to see them.

With delight Margaret sorted out the twelve best photographs which she had taken in the steel mill and hurried to Mr. Kulas' office. When he looked at the photographs, he exclaimed happily, "Never have pictures like these been taken anywhere in steel mills before."

A Surprise Opportunity

TAKING PHOTOGRAPHS of steel making set the stage for an unexpected change in Margaret's career. The Otis Steel Company bought and distributed many of her photographs and even published them in a book, *The Story of Steel*. Copies of her photographs also appeared in newspapers and magazines in different parts of the country. Several large manufacturing companies in the Midwest called her to inquire whether she would be interested in taking photographs in their factories.

In the spring of 1929 she was surprised to receive a telegram which read: "Have seen your steel photographs. Can you come to New York within a week at our expense? Henry R. Luce, *Time* magazine."

Happily Margaret hurried down the street to show the telegram to Mr. Bemis. "See what I have," she shouted, waving the telegram.

She handed the telegram to Mr. Bemis, who read it hurriedly but carefully. "That sounds wonderful," he said. "I'm glad that you have come to the attention of *Time*."

"Yes, that seems good, but I don't know what the telegram means," said Margaret. "From what I remember of *Time*, it contains very few illustrations except on the cover."

"Have you seen a copy of *Time* lately?" asked Mr. Bemis. "Possibly it has changed its policy and includes more photographs now."

Margaret rushed to the library to look at late copies of *Time*. She was fascinated with the beautiful covers on the magazine but found only a few photographs on the inside. As she examined the copies, she pondered over her future. She thought of all the factories, smoke-stacks, barges, railroad trains, and bridges she would photograph if she continued her present career. "No," she thought, "I can't go to New York and give up all these things."

She went back to talk with Mr. Bemis. "I've examined the latest copies of *Time* and there has been no change in its policy," she said. "The covers are beautiful, but there are only a few photographs on the inside. I wouldn't be happy to give up industrial photography. For this reason there's no point in my going to New York for an interview."

"Don't decide so quickly," advised Mr. Bemis. "I think you should accept the invita-tion to find out what Mr. Luce has in mind. Maybe the magazine is planning a new policy."

"I guess you're right," said Margaret. "I'll

take some of my photographs along to show Mr. Luce, and perhaps a few other persons, too. Then possibly I'll be able to sell a few photographs while I'm there."

"Fine," said Mr. Bemis. "It always pays to investigate. Something good may come of this. With your talent you have nothing to fear."

Later that week Margaret went to New York for her interview with Mr. Luce. Neatly dressed and carrying her portfolio under her arm, she walked into the magazine office. Mr. Luce greeted her warmly and introduced her to one of his associates. Then he began to ask her questions. Was she a professional photographer or did she take photographs as a hobby? Did she have a studio? Did she have another job? Why did she take photographs of a steel mill? Margaret could barely keep up with Mr. Luce in answering his questions.

"Yes, I'm a professional photographer and I

take photographs to earn a living," she explained. "I have a studio and spend all my time in photography. I have no other job. I took the photographs in the steel mill because I love industrial photography."

Mr. Luce looked at her and smiled. She could tell from the expression on his face that he was pleased with her answers. Without wasting more time, he told her why he had invited her to come to New York. He explained that he planned to start a magazine, *Fortune*, to be devoted to business and industry.

Then he looked at Margaret intently and said, "We plan to make photographs a major part of the stories in our magazine. We want to have a photographer and writer work together in preparing the stories. Now you can understand why we have asked you to come here. We think you are well suited to the special kind of program we have in mind."

Margaret was elated and her eyes shone brightly. Never in her wildest dreams had she ever expected to have such an opportunity. It seemed nothing short of a miracle that this offer should come to her now. It was coming right at the time when she was beginning her career in industrial photography.

Mr. Luce wanted her to start work at an early date and she readily agreed. The first issue of *Fortune* wouldn't be published for eight months, but he wanted her to help get a supply of photographs and story materials ready in advance. She and different writers would have to travel to various parts of the country to prepare the stories firsthand.

She felt so overjoyed that she wrote her mother, "I feel as if the world has been opened up and I hold all the keys."

At present the managing editor, Parker Lloyd-Smith, was preparing a dummy or sample copy of the magazine for advertising purposes. He asked Margaret whether he might include some of her steel mill photographs and she readily consented. The dummy met with a favorable response.

On Margaret's first assignment she was to take photographs of the shoemaking industry. On this assignment, she and a writer traveled to Lynn, Massachusetts, by boat. There they covered every step of shoemaking from the tanning of leather to putting shoes into boxes.

Margaret's next industrial subject to explore was glass-making. To cover this subject, she traveled to Corning, New York, where she and a writer visited a company making electric light bulbs. There they not only explored the making of bulbs by machinery but found the remnants of the old method of glass blowing. A man puffed up his cheeks and blew hot glass nuggets into large light bulbs.

Next Margaret and a writer made a quick trip to New Jersey, where she was much surprised to find that orchids begin their lives in test tubes rather than flower beds. The next day she took off to New London, Connecticut, to study the fishing industry. There she climbed huge piles of fresh fish to take photographs. There also she and the writer obtained a story about refrigeration which soon would revolutionize the whole food industry.

Another assignment took Margaret to Chicago, where she helped Mr. Lloyd-Smith, the managing editor, prepare a story on the meat packing industry. They visited the Chicago stockyards, where she photographed farm animals which had been shipped from farms in the Midwest. They traced the hog packing industry from the live animals to the finished pork products. They discovered that in the hog packing industry nearly everything was used.

Shortly before the new magazine was to start publication Mr. Luce decided to prepare a story on South Bend, Indiana, as an industrial center. There he and Margaret explored everything from the making of toys and fishing tackle to the manufacture of farm machinery and automobiles. One day when they visited a foundry, an accident occurred and molten metal started to splatter all over the floor. Quickly Mr. Luce dashed forward and grabbed Margaret's camera just in time to save it.

Margaret's next assignment for *Fortune*, which was entirely different, took her to Boston to photograph a new bank building. With the help of an electrician, she decided to take her photographs at night when the bank would be free of people. When she reached the bank, however, even though the doors were closed, she found all the bank officials there. They were running about with worried looks on their

faces and seemed to have little patience with her. Finally she asked one of them, "Why all the scurrying here and there tonight?"

"Haven't you read tonight's paper?" he asked. "The stock market has failed and the bottom has dropped out of everything."

This was Margaret's first introduction to the panic of 1929. From then on, banks, factories, and other business places across the country began to close their doors. This was a difficult time to start a new magazine, but Mr. Luce and the others decided to proceed.

In the early days of the depression Margaret was sent to Newport, Rhode Island, to photograph the America's Cup Races. On the day before the first race she went out in a boat to take photographs of the boats which were practicing for the races. Suddenly her boat overturned and she was tossed out with her camera. She bobbed up and down in the water, trying to save both herself and her camera. Finally, after about ten minutes of violent struggle, another boat came to rescue her from the tossing water. When she reached shore and recovered from her ordeal, she discovered that her camera was ruined. This meant that she wouldn't be able to take photographs of the cup races.

One of her greatest thrills came when she was asked to photograph the Chrysler Building, which was under construction in New York. She realized that this assignment would be both difficult and dangerous, because the Chrysler Building was to be the tallest in the city. Sometimes, in sub-freezing weather, she had to climb eight hundred feet to a tower which swayed as much as eight feet in the wind.

Frequently the welders and riveters paused in their work to watch this girl photographer climb out on steel girders with her camera to shoot the photographs she wanted. "Be care-

160

ful," one of them called loudly to warn her. "Just don't look down. Imagine that you're only eight feet instead of eight hundred feet above the ground."

When the workmen completed the 61st floor of the building they started to build a steel structure which extended out from the building. Margaret was so fascinated by this structure that she decided to move her Bourke-White Studio to one of the top floors. She had two terraces where she could step out and look over the city far below her.

On one of the terraces she started a small collection of animals, including alligators and turtles. Inside the studio she had a tropical fish tank or aquarium built into one of the walls. She collected egg cases of praying mantises and watched them carefully as they hatched one after another.

The Bourke-White Studio now had a staff of

eight people. In its new location it began to specialize in advertising photography. In this kind of photography it is necessary to make things look as good as possible.

For advertising purposes, Margaret took photographs of nearly everything from automobiles to chewing gum and often had amusing experiences. Once she attempted to take a photograph of a strawberry mousse, a frozen gelatin-like dessert. Just as she started to shoot the mousse, it collapsed over the plate.

On another occasion she had to take a photograph for a hair restorer company. One of her photographs was supposed to show a man completely bald and the same man with a full head of hair. She couldn't find a man who was willing to have his head shaved for the bald picture. Finally she solved her problem by getting a prisoner in a lockup who was willing to have his head shaved for a small fee.

From Machines to People

DURING MARGARET'S early years in New York her activities were wide and various. She spent half her time on story assignments for *Fortune* and the other half on advertising photography for her Bourke-White Studio. She was always glad when the time came to take photographs for *Fortune*.

Her assignments for this magazine took her all over the world. Some of them lasted for only a few days and others for weeks and months. She loved to travel in new and different places, meet other people, and find out how they lived and worked.

163

One of her assignments took her to Germany to photograph different types of industry. She took photographs of steel mills and huge munition factories in the Ruhr Valley and elsewhere. In addition she took photographs of tanks, war planes, and men taking military training. Later *Fortune* published her photographs to show that Germany, now under the rule of Adolf Hitler, once again was preparing for war.

From Germany *Fortune* wanted her to proceed to the Soviet Union, but she had difficulty making the necessary arrangements. Up to that time no outside photographers had been allowed to enter the country. Therefore it took months of government negotiations to obtain the needed permissions.

Altogether she made three short trips to the Soviet Union. On her first two trips she took photographs of steel mills, manufacturing plants, power plants, and all kinds of machinery at work. On her third trip she decided to visit a rural area to see how the peasants lived and worked. For this purpose she chose the Socialist Republic of Georgia, in the southern part of the country bordering the Black Sea. This area was especially interesting because it was the boyhood home of Joseph Stalin, then head ruler of the Soviet Union.

The ruler of Georgia, or President, and his assistants called Commissars worked out the plans for Margaret's visit and later decided to travel with her. All of them rode horseback and Margaret had an extra horse to carry her equipment. They slept in caves at night and depended upon the peasants for much of their food. The people greeted them warmly and many villagers sang songs to entertain them.

One day in their travels they came to the small village where Joseph Stalin had been born. His birthplace was a little mud hut with an earthen floor and a hole in the roof to let the smoke escape. Margaret took photographs of both the village and the hut.

In 1934 when Margaret returned to America she found an entirely different type of assignment awaiting her. She was sent to take photographs in the midwestern part of our country, which had been plagued with a destructive drought. For months there had been no rain in this part of the country and the area had come to be known as the "Great Dust Bowl."

Margaret chartered a small airplane so that she could cover the drought area as rapidly as possible. This airplane was only a frail two-seater, but it could land almost any place she wanted to go. The pilot, who was a stunt flyer at county fairs, was well acquainted with this part of the country. He could fly Margaret to the right place in the right sunlight to take the special shots that she wanted.

She was stunned by what she saw as she toured the dry, barren region. There were miles of thirsty land parched by the blistering sun. Drooping wisps of corn withered in the baked earth. Rivers of sand flowed in streams where formerly there were brooks of clear running water. Windmills turned in the dusty wind but had no water to pump. Huge clouds of dust moved across the land.

Margaret was shocked by the appearance of the land but even more shocked by the looks on the faces of the people. She was grieved to see persons who had no way to overcome their misfortune. Strong farmers and their hard-working wives were sad and defeated. All they could do was watch their farmland blow away.

Margaret's experiences in the Dust Bowl helped to bring about a great change in her interests in photography. Up to now, she had been fascinated with the fantasy of factories and machines. Now suddenly she became concerned with people and their problems.

When she returned to her studio in New York she found that it had agreed to make photographs of automobile tires for advertising purposes. She watched as an assistant made a phony setup with tires carved out of wood splashing through gooey mud made from clay. After she photographed this setup she shook her head and slumped into a chair. Somehow taking this photograph seemed terribly shallow and weak after photographing the horrified looks on the faces of people in the Dust Bowl.

A few days later she spent long hours photographing automobiles for an advertisement. She took shots of them from all directions under different lights to bring out sharp colors and other details. That evening, after she returned to her apartment, she ate a simple supper and went to bed early.

An hour or so later she was overcome by a terrible dream. She dreamed that a horde of ugly shapes was rushing after her. No matter where she went this ugly horde of shapes surrounded her. They moved toward her with their giant hoods raised like threatening jaws. Then she recognized them as the automobiles which she had been photographing that day.

She started to run and they took after her. She stumbled and fell. At this moment she awoke and found herself lying on the floor. She had fallen out of bed trying to escape from the ugly shapes in her dream.

The following morning as she ate breakfast on the terrace of her apartment, she looked down at the street far below her. There she noticed people hurrying along in all directions on their way to work. She wondered where all of them were going and what they were going to do during the coming hours. Now she realized that she had to take photographs of real people and real things in a real world.

Later that day, when she went to her studio, she received an urgent telephone call from an advertising agency. "We want you to take five color photographs for us and we'll pay you an unusual price for them," said the speaker.

The speaker explained fully what the photographs were to be like and what price the agency would pay for them. Margaret hesitated because she had never had such a good offer before. Then at last she mustered up enough courage to say, "No, I'm not interested."

Following this decision she sat down on the floor with her elbows on her knees and her chin in her hands. She pondered in deep thought. Now that she had decided what she would not do, she had to decide what she would do. One thing was sure to her, she wanted to photograph people rather than mere machines.

Cotton Country
to Air Raids

WITHIN A WEEK or so after Margaret decided that she wanted to photograph people rather than machines, she had a surprise opportunity. A prominent author, Erskine Caldwell, invited her to take photographs for a new book which he was planning to write. As author and photographer they would work together in creating a book about people living in the cotton and tobacco growing regions of the Deep South.

Mr. Caldwell made all the arrangements for the tour. He and Margaret were to meet in mid-June, 1936, in Augusta, Georgia, to start their unusual type of explorations. He arranged for a secretary to travel with them to take notes and to keep records.

Before the time came for Margaret to leave New York for the Deep South she had a second surprise opportunity. She was invited to become a member of the staff for a new magazine to be called *Life*. This magazine, which was to be started by *Time* and *Fortune*, would emphasize photographs in presenting the news.

Margaret felt very excited about being included in the birth of this new type of magazine. Fortunately, accepting this offer wouldn't interfere with her plans to help illustrate the book for Mr. Caldwell. She was overjoyed by the good fortune which surrounded her.

When the time came to leave for Augusta, Georgia, she set off with an enormous stack of luggage. She had suitcases, cameras, tripods, lighting equipment, films, and two glass jars, each containing a praying mantis egg case. She took these glass jars along because she was eager to photograph the life cycle of this dramatic insect. She kept the jars on the seat beside her to be sure they were safe.

In traveling through the South, Margaret and Mr. Caldwell tried to interview people where they actually lived and worked. They drove along back country roads and stopped to talk with people in fields, at barns, and on the front porches of homes. Day after day they climbed out of their automobile and ambled over to a fence to talk with a farmer. At first the farmer usually eyed them with suspicion, but fortunately Mr. Caldwell spoke with an easy southern drawl. This led the farmer to trust them and to answer their questions more freely.

In one sharecropper's cabin Margaret met a little girl named Begonia. "How many brothers and sisters have you?" she asked.

"I have heaps of them," answered Begonia.

"How many?" asked Margaret. "Do you have eight? Do you have ten?"

Begonia just shook her head. "I don't know, ma'am. I've never counted them."

Later the little girl revealed that among all the other children in the family she had a twin sister. She and this sister took turns going to school every other day because they had only one pair of shoes and one coat between them. In her travels Margaret found many other children not only destitute of clothing but even lacking enough food to eat.

As she and Mr. Caldwell traveled, she kept watching the praying mantis egg cases in her glass jars. Finally the magic day arrived and she let out a cry of joy. "Stop the car! The miracle is about to happen!" Mr. Caldwell stopped the car promptly and she took photographs of the little green midgets as they came fluttering from the eggs.

After Margaret and Mr. Caldwell finished their trip through the Deep South, they returned to New York. There they organized their stories and photographs into the form of a book, called *You Have Seen Their Faces*. Almost overnight this book became popular and was widely read in all parts of the country.

About this time Margaret received her first assignment for the new magazine *Life*. Mr. Luce, the editor, sent her to Montana to photograph the construction of Fort Peck Dam, the largest earth-filled dam in the world. Her dramatic photograph of this dam was used as the cover picture for the first issue of *Life* November 23, 1936. The first story inside the magazine was an account which she had written about the people who lived in the ramshackle town where the dam was being built.

As photographer for *Life* magazine, she never knew what or where her next assignment would be. She was sent all over the world to photograph people and places. On one occasion, during the summer, she was sent to Canada to accompany Lord Tweedsmuir, the Governor-General, on a trip to the Arctic Circle. When she left, she took along ten butterfly cocoons which would hatch before long.

When she reached Canada, she boarded a ship with the Governor-General and his party to sail northward. On board ship she taped the cocoons to the rail of the upper deck. Then she got her camera ready to photograph the butterflies whenever they emerged.

A few days later, as the ship neared the Arctic Circle, she noticed signs that the cocoons would soon break open. With her camera ready she sat down in a deck chair to wait and to watch. When the moment came, the ship's captain stopped the ship so that its movements wouldn't interfere with her taking pictures.

During the next half hour the ship remained still while she photographed the beautiful butterflies emerging from the cocoons. Now once more the captain started the ship and said, "In thirty years I have never stopped the ship for anything like this."

On another occasion Margaret accompanied Mr. Caldwell to Germany, which still was under the control of Adolf Hitler. There they gathered information on Germany's preparations for war. After they returned they wrote a book called *North of the Danube* based on their findings.

By now Mr. Caldwell and Margaret had become close friends and decided to get married. In 1941, soon after their marriage, they left on a trip to the Soviet Union. Since much of Europe was already engaged in World War II, they had to fly westward across the Pacific Ocean and the continent of Asia in order to reach the Soviet Union. Exactly one month after they arrived in Moscow, the country was suddenly invaded by Germany.

At once the American Ambassador to the Soviet Union called them to the Embassy office. He explained that it was his duty to protect American citizens traveling in the Soviet Union, since the country was being invaded by Germany. "I can put you on a train bound for the border if you wish to leave," he said. "Nobody knows how soon Moscow will be bombed, but it is almost sure to happen. In case you wish to stay, I'll give you all the help I can."

Mr. Caldwell and Margaret decided to stay on. Soon the German bombers came and everybody was forced to go to bomb shelters for safety. From here Margaret was disappointed because she couldn't see or photograph what was taking place. Finally she and Mr. Caldwell decided to move from their hotel to the American Embassy for a few days. There she would be permitted to stay above ground to photograph nightly bombing raids as they occurred.

One night at the Embassy she watched the searchlights cross and recross the sky trying to spot German planes. Suddenly she sensed that a bomb was coming in her direction and threw herself on the floor for protection. Almost immediately she was covered with shattered glass from the broken windows in the room, but fortunately she was not injured.

In photographing the air raids, she discovered that she needed to use several cameras in order to obtain photographs. She placed the cameras so that they pointed in different directions to cover as much of the sky as possible. Then she constantly had to be ready to shoot the right camera at the right time.

A War Correspondent

WHEN THE United States entered World War II, Margaret felt that in some way she had to be of service to her country. The magazine *Life* worked out arrangements with military authorities in Washington, D.C., for her to become a war correspondent. She would be attached to the U.S. Air Corps, and would take photographs which would be useful both to *Life* and military authorities. In this new position she would become the first woman war correspondent in the entire history of the country.

Her decision was hard to make because right at this time Mr. Caldwell had an offer to go to Hollywood. Now it would be impossible for her to accompany him, so they decided to separate. Even though they came to this decision, they remained close friends from then on.

Since Margaret was to become the first woman war correspondent, the military authorities had to design a special uniform for her. They decided to follow the general pattern of an officer's uniform, except that she would wear either skirts or slacks, depending on the occasions. On the shoulders of her coat she would wear a war correspondent's insignia.

She began service by flying to England. Soon after she arrived, she went to London to photograph Winston Churchill, Prime Minister of England, on his sixty-eighth birthday. This photograph of the Prime Minister was used on the cover of an early issue of *Life*.

One of the crew members at the bomber base where Margaret was stationed asked her to select a name for their bomber. She looked at the names on some of the other bombers and suggested the name *Flying Flitgun*. The men liked her suggestion and painted the name in large letters on the sides of the bomber. Then they painted a yellow flitgun spraying three insects with the faces of Hitler, Mussolini, and Hirohito. Finally they printed Peggy, Margaret's nickname, on one of the engines, which was a real tribute because they usually named the engines after their wives or sweethearts. Finally they invited Margaret to break a bottle of Coke over the bomber to christen it.

Before long the bombers were sent to a new base in North Africa to help with an invasion. Margaret asked to go along for the bombing, and her request was granted. The General, however, ordered her to go by ship because of the danger of traveling by airplane.

The airplanes reached North Africa safely,

but Margaret's ship was torpedoed. She was asleep in her bunk at night when the torpedo hit and was thrown to the floor. Trembling with fear, she hastily scrambled into her clothes, grabbed her bag and camera and started for the lifeboat station.

She found the lifeboat half filled with water. As soon as the boat was loaded, it was lowered into the tossing waters of the sea. Some of the lifeboats which had already been lowered over-turned when they hit the water. People from these boats were struggling about in the water trying to save themselves.

As Margaret looked at these frantic persons she spotted a nurse close by the lifeboat. She held out her hand and tried to rescue the nurse from the threatening waves. At last others joined her and together they were able to drag the nurse into the boat.

By this time the boat was so weighted down

with people and water that it was in danger of sinking. Everyone looked at one another, wondering what to do. "Let's bail out the water with our helmets," said Margaret. "We'll have to work together in rhythm in order to keep out of the way of the men who are rowing. Some of us can dip water and others pour it out."

As they dipped and poured the water from the boat, they began to sing a popular song, "You Are My Sunshine, My Only Sunshine." Then others from nearby lifeboats joined in singing this same song. The singing seemed to give a feeling of courage to the people floundering about in the water. A soldier, who was swimming toward a nearby raft, held up his hand and shouted, "Hey, taxi!" An American nurse who was swimming in her lifejacket called out, "Which way to North Africa?"

"Take the third wave to the left," answered a nurse from the lifeboat.

After Margaret reached Africa, General James H. (Jimmy) Doolittle, the commanding officer, invited her to go on a bombing mission. "Thank you, General," Margaret said. "That's exactly what I wanted to do."

At sunrise the next morning briefings were held for the mission. The battle formation included thirty-two bombers and Margaret was allowed to fly in the lead bomber. As soon as the bombers were in the air she began to take photographs. Before long they were over the target and she could see the anti-aircraft fire from below. As the bomber twisted and turned in the air to avoid anti-aircraft fire, it gave her all the angles she needed for taking the exact photographs she wanted.

As she looked down she saw plumes of black and white smoke tinged with red, caused by American bombs exploding on the enemy target. Then, here and there in the air, she spotted gleaming, spidery forms, the ack-ack from anti-aircraft guns trying to halt the raid.

Later Margaret learned that this was a very important raid. It helped to drive the German forces in North Africa back to the continent of Europe. This was one of the first major steps toward winning the war.

From North Africa Margaret, traveling by jeep, ship, and airplane, returned to America. While here she delivered some of her photographs to the War Department in Washington and others to *Life* magazine in New York. Later *Life* published her story entitled "Life's Bourke-White Goes Bombing."

About six months later she went to Italy to participate in the Allied Forces' ground campaign. There she rode in jeeps and hiked through the slushy mud with the troops. Finally she combined her photographs with a story to be published in a book, *Purple Heart Valley*.

In the spring of 1945, when the war was coming to a close, Margaret flew to Germany, where she joined the American forces along the River Rhine. There she remained until the war came to an end. Following the war she prepared an illustrated story for *Life* magazine on the Krupp Munitions Works which supplied Germany with much of its munitions.

After World War II *Life* sent Margaret to India in southern Asia, where she worked off and on until 1948. During this period she became closely acquainted with Mahatma Gandhi, the dramatic spiritual leader of India at that time. From photographs and notes she published a book called *Halfway to Freedom*.

Later she was sent by *Life* to prepare an article on the gold mines of South Africa. There she followed two men who worked in the mines and photographed their activities. At times she went with them deep underground to one of the most dangerous parts of the mine to photograph them while carrying on their work.

In 1952, while the Korean War was in progress, *Life* sent Margaret to South Korea. She traveled about the country by helicopter, which dropped her off in different places. Then she traveled by herself except for the protection of the local police.

Her greatest danger on this trip came from terrorists who hid in the mountains and came down to conduct guerrilla warfare. In all her war experiences she had never run into guerrillas before. Little did she realize how much fear and destruction of life they could cause. Since she was a photographer, she faced grave danger of becoming one of their victims.

Her trip to Korea was one of her last assignments for *Life*. About this time she was stricken with illness which prevented her from carrying on her customary strenuous activities. From then on she battled her illness until the time of her death in 1971.

Margaret Bourke-White was a woman of unusual ability, energy, and courage. From this background of qualities she carved for herself an outstanding career. At the height of this career she was one of the most widely traveled and widely known persons in the world.

Her record of achievements was marked by a number of firsts. She was the first woman to attempt industrial photography. She was the first woman to become a successful news photographer. She was the first woman ever to become a war correspondent.

Margaret Bourke-White's works will long live after her. Through her photographs, books, magazine articles, and other writings she has left a vivid picture of the world as it really is.